THE VOICE OF THE BRAIN OF BRITAIN

A PORTRAIT OF RADIO FOUR

BY
KEVIN D'ARCY

RAJAH BOOKS

First published
in the United Kingdom
in 2007
by Rajah Books
40 Bruce Road
London E3 3HL
020 8981 4691
rajahbooks@btopenworld.com

ISBN : 978-0-9556706-0-2

Printed and bound in Great Britain by
Biddles Ltd, King's Lynn, Norfolk

About the author:

Kevin d'Arcy worked for the BBC for two decades, as well as writing on media for The Economist, and for five years published Spokesman, the quarterly international review of communicating policy.

This book
is dedicated
to every listener
to Radio Four

CONTENTS

CONTENTS

The motivation

Like any other portrait, this is strictly a personal perspective, but one shared, I hope, by many others who might be just as surprised as myself that such a key part of the British psyche has been so underrecorded.

The inspiration to try this as a book was, as is often the case, an accident. I was one day routinely reviewing a talk I had just given about British media to foreign civil servants, as a way of explaining how press officers here must analyse their targets. In many ways there is little difference between different countries in this. But there is a big difference in the way that speech radio can have an influence, not just on its own audience, but also on other forms of media. And in Britain speech radio, as everyone knows, is primarily Radio Four.

Writing this book is also selfish. My mother avoided discussing my embarrassing habit of journalism with anyone until, one day, she was stopped in the street and congratulated by relative strangers on her son's appearance on Radio Four that morning. Suddenly she came to believe that what I did may - just - be worthwhile.

Another factor was Alastair Cook. I broadcast a Letter from London for a while, inspired by him but, of course, overshadowed. When I asked him, in New York, how I might get his job he recommended that I push him off a bridge, as he had no plans to retire. I hesitated. And just as well. But he and thousands of others like him who have made speech radio in Britain what it is, deserve to have their collective contribution to a national culture marked.

However, I was determined not to go down the road so well defined by others. It seemed to me that there were quite enough books published about the BBC from the inside, but nothing very much about the BBC from the outside. So discovering how decisions about programming are made, and especially how they reflected the needs and tastes of the audience, could be quite rewarding.

It is obvious that radio is the most intimate of all media. And as the audiences for print and television media fall in Britain, it looks like becoming the most important new media. And, after all, when something like Radio Four becomes a part of your personal lifestyle - not to mention, if you also have television, having to pay for it through a compulsory tax - there seems at least a democratic right to know about how it works.

&

The subject

Talking or writing about Radio Four is for many people like talking or writing about your best friend. It is slightly embarrassing. For some is it a declaration of love. For others, simply a statement of respect or affection.

But, above everything, it is an embodiment of something special, above the ordinary. It is normally something that helps to raise you above the toil and trouble of everyday life. It might be a friendly and familiar companion, at home or on the road. Or it could be that essential something extra that, if nothing else, defines a truth.

Outside of Britain, this country is admired, in order of importance, for the Queen, for football, for the BBC. And Radio Four (I respectfully submit, ma'am) is the essence of the BBC.

Personally, I look back nearly a century - yes, before I was born - to the writing of the extremely perceptive H L Mencken, a third generation German Jewish journalist who probably did more than anyone else to shake the United States into an awareness of culture. On the one hand, he lambasted the pathetic standard of radio journalism in that country, on the other he lamented the almost total inability of his compatriots to formulate original ideas. In 1928 he wrote about a radio set he was given that 'I have made probably 250 attempts to get something out of it that was worth hearing. But although I have tackled it from all hours of daylight to 2 am and swept the pointer from end to end of the dial, I can't recall more than 30 occasions when I have got anything remotely describable as civilised entertainment'.

I would suggest that the world has not moved on a great deal since then. I have worked in the US for a number of years and suggest that comparison is useful. If the megalomania of the United States owes its position to anything it is due to the ignorance and, hence, indifference of its electorate - and so the enforced position of its politicians, who inevitably influence the rest of the world - due entirely to the passivity of its journalists.

Outside of elitist magazines, US journalists generally seem little more able now to ask thoughtful or penetrating questions of their elected leaders than they were in the days of HLM. As before, the social and political agenda is all about conformity. Thank goodness, this is not true in Britain, largely because of the BBC and mainly Radio Four. Sorry to sound prissy, but there you go.

It is quite true, however, that ambition for excellence is rare, and ambition for excellence beyond materialism is especially rare. Radio Four, I suggest, embodies that. It is for those who love the idea of ideas. Isn't that a great idea?

&

The threat

Yes, it is a possibility. That this constant companion, the voice of the brain of Britain known otherwise as Radio Four might one day be no longer available to us, in Britain or anywhere else.

The quickest way for anyone to lose grip of it, obviously, is to simply leave the country. Yes, of course there is the internet, where much of the output can be heard around the world, but not without some awkwardness. And that is not the kind of relationship that most of us prefer. The talk radio we love is always with us – in the car, the bed, the bath, the kitchen, or driving down the road.

The other way of losing grip of it is, quite simply, to have forces beyond our control try to take it away from us, either for political or financial reasons. It happens all the time. People who make use of it to promote their own efforts are always keen to change the rules of entry, which naturally can effect the product.

Political press officers telephoning the editors of the Today programme set a well-known example. And remember, the public relations business is usually better staffed and financed than journalism. Which means that every time the BBC has to renegotiate the existence and size of the licence fee - designed to fund all of its output, of course, of which radio gets just a small part - the finance available to put into programmes comes under threat again.

And it is not so long since the BBC's chairman and director general both resigned because of the Hutton report on Radio Four's Today programme, persuaded to do so by the board of governors, only to be followed by the board themselves, who were then replaced by a trust (trust?). Overseas admirers of the BBC and its famous tradition for independence were almost as stunned as the staff themselves at such blatant interference.

But if, as a result of political pressure, the standard of reporting falls, the target audience would also lose interest, eventually leading to the kind of programming that no politician would want to join – thus killing the golden goose.

So let's look at how it began.

&

PAST

In the beginning

There was no immaculate conception, of course. However much reverence listeners to Radio Four may hold for their soul mate, the truth is that the network grew organically, from various directions, from various roots. Radio Four is simply what it is now.

In the beginning there was just the BBC, the initials then representing not a corporation, but the British Broadcasting Company. And the beginning, of course, was soon after the invention of radio, and long, long before the present luxuriant growth of terrestrial television, satellite broadcasting and on-line communication.

Just over a century ago one Guglielmo Marconi convinced the world that sounds could fly and land through the ether with a bit of organised persuasion, and in Britain this was legitimised by the passing of a parliamentary Act in 1904, giving the Postmaster General responsibility for organising it in the public interest. Marconi's invention of radio transmitters and receivers was then passed on to the Marconi Scientific Instrument Co. Ltd which received permission to regularly broadcast in February 1920, using the station named 2LO.

Immediately there were protests from other companies that had gone swiftly into the business of making radio equipment -

such as Radio Communication, Metropolitan Vickers, Western Electric, British Thompson Houston and the General Electric Company - and it was obvious to the Post Office that giving one company a broadcasting monopoly was wrong. So all of them were invited to form a consortium with Marconi, which they did, and this became the BBC in November 1922.

It is interesting to note that the Postmaster General's role was initially seen as ensuring that individuals sending individual messages to each other did not interfere with military use of the airwaves. Then, as now, the main reason for governmental control over the use of the limited amount of airwaves (as opposed to unregulated print media) was for national security reasons. It took businessmen to recognise that broadcasting - or the wireless - could also be a system of mass communication potentially as important as newspapers.

The press barons of the day were important early influences

Eventually the press barons became equally interested. The Canadian owner of the Daily Express, Max Beaverbrook, formed the 80,000 member Wireless League, as a means of influencing the output of the BBC, ostensibly on behalf of listeners, while Lord Drogheda of the Financial Times formed the equally influential 1,000 member Wireless Association, but mainly inspired by manufacturers and technical enthusiasts.

It was agreed that the Post Office would collect an annual licence fee from owners of radio receivers on behalf of the BBC and that this, together with some initial finance from the manufacturers, plus a tax on the sale of receivers, would be used to fund the venture. The main exceptions to this agreeable state of affairs were companies importing radios. They preferred not to agree.

Of course the British experience was not, until then, unique. Broadcasting by telephone, for instance, had begun in Hungary in 1893. A company called Telefon Hirmondo started daily broadcasts then and had collected 6,000 subscribers within five years. Radio broadcasting began in the USA in 1921, but politicians there decided in the Radio Act of 1927 that public money should not be involved, meaning that broadcasting, all financed by advertising, was left virtually uncontrolled. One result of that was serious overlap on the airwaves between the many broadcasters, until the Federal Communications Commission was set up in 1936. It was an equally free market in other developed countries at the time, but British legislators felt certain that they should not follow that route.

All the same, in Britain it was clear that paying for a licence could be little more than a voluntary act on behalf of a grateful audience, if only because there was no effective system for enforcement. By 1923 the Post Office had issued some 80,000 licences, although receiver sales suggested that four times as many as that were listening. By 1924 about a million licences were valid, but five million sets had been sold.

The very first receivers were individually usable crystal sets, selling for between two to four pounds. More widely accessible valve sets with loud speakers were soon to follow, although they were to cost considerably more, in some cases twice the national average annual income, which was £80 in 1937. And this was a major reason for radio use then – and for a very long time after – being seen as a mainly middle class activity. Not until 1939, at the start of the second world war, were so-called utility sets available for £6, which also coincided with more widely attractive programming.

Price was just one limitation on the sale of sets. The other limitation was need. Radio was little more than an amusing pastime in its early years.

The man who founded the Daily Mail in the same year as Marconi registered his broadcasting invention, was Alfred Harmsworth (later Lord Northcliffe) and he hit on the first good idea for promoting radio in 1920 when he suggested that the famous singer Dame Nellie Melba be invited to broadcast a concert. The Post Office was persuaded that this had been a frivolous use of the airwaves, so imposed a ban on such things soon afterwards.

Originally, anyone seriously interested in local, national or world affairs would get what they wanted from newspapers. This established advantage of the printed media was reinforced (with the aid of lobbying from the Newspaper Publishers Association) by forbidding the BBC from broadcasting anything resembling news before the early evening. The afternoon papers sold in substantial numbers and were nervous of their market share. The morning papers were equally nervous of their right to announce the day.

But the rot had already set in, so to speak, if only because as early as in 1923 retailers selling radio receivers had discovered a good promotional wheeze by placing a set in front of the shop in the evening, to attract the attention of workers coming home. Sports results and racing summaries were especially popular. National events such as the Boat Race and the FA Cup Final could attract a crowd of 800 outside of a single shop – thus beginning, by the way, a continual encouragement by broadcasters for an increase in national, as opposed to regional, identity by concentrating on national events.

Music from the radio got people dancing in the streets

Music also attracted audiences. In 1923 The Oxford Wireless Telephone Company took a receiver by truck to an open air event at Henley which was reported thus by the Oxford Chronicle: "The reality of the reception may be realised when it is known that a large portion of the audience actually clapped and applauded . . . The dance music was so greatly appreciated and was so loud and distinct that many couples danced to it."

But the big breakthrough in BBC news coverage was created by the national strike of 1926. The strike meant, among other things, that there were no national newspapers, so there was no other way of communicating with the public but through radio. The ban on daytime news was suspended and bulletins went out at 10am, 1pm, 4pm, 7pm and 9.30pm. Even those on strike depended on them, as the unions had not planned for any communication system of their own.

Typically, in West London, teams of secretaries, working on relays at Chiswick Town Hall, were taking down transcripts of bulletins in shorthand and typing them for display outside. Radio shop owners were also displaying typed bulletins in their windows, to help reinforce the value of their products. Traditional London clubs broke their normal code of silence by installing radios in halls and libraries. And those few newspapers that had not joined the strike, but could get no information from their normal sources, also used the BBC as an authority on the news.

The main problem was the value of the bulletins, which generally followed the government line, as this is where most bulletins began. The BBC's own newsgathering ability was limited: either to government hand-outs or to news agency copy, which was often little different. There was not even a dedicated news department until 1934. So this was the first of many situations where the BBC has had to decide on how impartial it could be without threatening the national interest. Unwillingly news-dependent strikers were especially bitter about this: but, all the same, when it came to an end, some 37,000 letters of thanks were sent for at least keeping the nation informed.

It was the general strike that gave news coverage its reputation

So a national crisis had turned the BBC into a national asset. An accident, perhaps, but crucial all the same. In 1927 the British Broadcasting Company was turned by Royal Charter into the nationally-owned but legally independent British Broadcasting Corporation, with the brief to inform, educate and entertain, but forbidden to carry advertisements or to express opinions. This was inspired by a committee of enquiry assembled to examine the BBCs declining financial health. The general manager, John Reith, became director general. Within two years the number of radio licences issued in Britain rose from two to nine million, while the BBC's long wave transmitter at Wrotham could reach 85 percent of the population.

Five years later, in 1932, the stately, white-stoned Broadcasting House was opened at the cusp of Portland Place, the Empire Service was launched as the first overseas network, and an ambitious National Programme was begun, in addition to the six existing regional services.

John Reith's ambitions for the BBC were typical of a man from a sternly moral, Scottish Calvinist background. He was out to improve peoples' minds. In the event, the output of each service consisted of a rotating mix of news, sport, drama, music, religion and entertainment, with the declared aim of surprising the listener with subjects they had not planned to hear, but which nevertheless might improve them. And it was welcomed.

Indeed, according to a writer in the New Statesman: "A good many people, I am sure, were charmed when, on the first day of the first general strike that this country has known, they turned to the wireless for news of what was happening to themselves and their civilisation and found themselves, having heard all the news that was fit to transmit, invited to listen to a talk on 'holidays with ants and grasshoppers.' Since Drake played out his game of bowls while the Armada was approaching, there have been few things more pleasantly characteristic of the English attitude to a crisis."

All the same, what how come to be called the Reithian attitude to broadcasting had its definite down-side. Especially on Sunday, when broadcasting was not allowed to start until half an hour past mid-day, with subjects restricted to religion, talks and (only) classical music.

Reith was aware of his critics. As he later (regally) wrote: "It is occasionally indicated to us that we are apparently setting out to give the public what we think they need – and not what they want – but few know what they want and very few what they need . . . In any case it is better to over-estimate the mentality of the public than to under-estimate it."

Also: "I think it will be admitted by all, that to have exploited so great a scientific invention for the purpose and pursuit to 'entertainment' alone would have been a prostitution of its powers and an insult to the character and intelligence of the people."

The reality was, however, that he, of all people, had no methodical way of telling what anyone thought - or knew - about anything. If it comes to that, Reith's claim to have seized the moral high ground should be clearly understood in context. The newspaper tycoon Max Beaverbrook was as anxious as anyone that the broadcasting monopoly should be used to raise the tone of what had then become a very sensational newspaper business. Also, Reith's own moral assumptions need to be considered alongside his personal behaviour. While he was dismissing women from his staff for getting married and men for getting divorced, he had for many years conducted an openly homosexual relationship up to and alongside his marriage. Flirtations with other women - some extremely young - were also not unknown.

There is considerable detail on this aspect of Reith's behaviour in the profile of him, The expense of glory, produced in 1993 by Ian Mcintyre, a previous controller of both Radios Four and Three, which drew heavily on Reith's diaries. It was clear that Reith had an extremely lonely childhood and subsequently found it hard to establish relationships. He was not immune to women, but seemed to have been much more drawn to men. One in particular, Charlie (David) Bower, he had been extremely close to for ten years and found it hard to abandon in favour of his wife, Muriel, which seemed to have led to a nervous breakdown after both Reith's and Bower's marriages. His diary recorded 'I love M very much but C was my love years before I knew her and I cannot let him go. He is all the world to me.' This was shortly before he joined the BBC. And only five years before that, while working in the US, his diary recorded meeting a Betty Stewart, who was 'ravishingly pretty and I feel

Reith's isolated childhood clearly produced a dislocated adult

greatly enamoured of her. She is really like a fairy princess.' Betty was twelve and half years old. These internal demons could not have helped in creating the necessary moral leadership of the BBC.

Moreover, competition - for the first of many times - forced a change on the BBC. Stations broadcasting to Britain from abroad such as Radio Luxembourg provided lighter fare than this, at least in the areas best able to hear them in the south and east of England, so started to steal the national audience. Until that time, the director general (in his opinion) had been the only listener officially recognised. But in 1936 – the year when regular television broadcasting began - he was finally persuaded by Sir Stephen Talents, the controller of public relations, largely in response to industry pressure, to commission research to measure the views of the British radio audience.

The most important listener was the director general

But as the man who then joined from the London Press Exchange to became the first head of audience research, Robert Silvey, afterwards recorded: 'In those days, the people who had wireless sets were not a cross-section of the whole population, it was a section of the population which had a pretty strong middle-class bias.'

Two years later Reith left his post - defeated, you might say, by the public need - though his influence lasted much longer than his tenure: horoscopes, gambling, jazz, swearing, sex: the list of forbidden subjects were legion. (Before the Second World War, in 1933, Reith had written in an internal memo: 'Germany has banned hot jazz and I'm sorry we should be behind in dealing with this filthy product of modernity.')

Stage two of the evolution was launched with a bang by the second world war. Like many other bodies in public life, the BBC found itself enrolled in promoting the national cause.

After the national strike had been won, daytime news bulletins had again disappeared, but on 25 August 1939, bulletins were again restored, at 10.30 am and 1 pm, in readiness for action. On August 21, the BBC had been asked to recall parliament, as well as school teachers, to prepare for the evacuation of all children out of London. On August 31 the evacuation was announced, and on the six o'clock news the fleet was mobilised. At 10.30 am the following day Britain heard of the fall of Poland.

The BBC moved what it could out of London and the airtime was filled with an awful lot of music. Such as the gallant Sandy MacPherson on his cinema organ, often playing as many as forty five sessions in a week. That, added to endless announcements of what to do in the event of an invasion, such as 'Making the most of a wartime larder' drove many to distraction. This was the time when the BBC first earned its nickname of 'Auntie'. (And the nickname was to be eagerly revived in the years to come by the emerging competition, often successfully inferring that every product of the BBC would be fussy and fusty.)

The regional networks were merged into one, for the military reason – not explained to the public – of reducing the number of detectable transmitters that might inadvertently be used to guide enemy aircraft. Its new name was the Home Service, but still the Reithian rule continued of rotating subjects. And so did the paternalistic lectures.

(In fact, BBC engineers quickly discovered a way of disabling the guidance value of their transmitters by having them randomly switch on and off and exchange information between themselves. All that the public knew about this was a variation in power output.)

Then, on 7 January, 1940, a programme was launched for the fighting forces, with the specific brief of maintaining morale. The troops had been asked to say what they wanted. They said variety shows, musical comedies and crooners. And that is what they got. Vera Lynn, the East End singer, was thrust upon a ready world and was soon named the forces sweetheart. Much binding in the Marsh was a comedy programme that ran for many years. Richard Murdoch, Kenneth Horne, Charlie Chester, Eric Barker and Jimmy Edwards all launched their long careers. Desert Island Discs began in January 1942 and Gardeners Question Time in April 1943 under it's original, rather coy, name of How does your garden grow?

The difficulty for the BBC was that all of this very popular output attracted a general audience half as big again as the principle Home Service. There was no alternative but to go with the flow. The Forces Programme became The Light Service (to be renamed The Light Programme after the war) and raising morale for the duration of the war became generally allowed.

There were questions in Parliament about the lowering of values, especially the broadcasting of Noel Coward singing his satirical 'Don't let's be beastly to the Germans' ('Let's be free with them and share the BBC with them'), but thankfully they led nowhere. Winston Churchill was particularly pleased. It was his favourite song.

More importantly, the creation of the Light Service marked the end of consecutive programmes and the start of parallel subject stations: stage three of the evolution.

Of course, a major change in the nature of all programming during the second world war, as in any war, was the strong increase in the need to know. Light music and humour may have been very necessary for the soul, but there was clearly a growing demand for information on the progress of the war (with an implied stress on the word 'progress') , matched only by the need of those in charge of the war to present what they considered to be the necessary (positive?) information.

Don't let's be beastly to the Germans, sang Coward

So this is when the BBC began to gradually take more initiative in collecting its own information. On D-Day on 6 June 1944 reporter Richard Dimbleby took one of the first portable recording machines into the battlefield. Broadcasting the sound of real gunfire was not welcomed by the government censors, but it eventually became acceptable. The art of the radio documentary was learned from the US experience of mixing factual information with dramatic reconstruction. And news was increasingly delivered with contextual comment.

Towards the end of the war, when the overseas General Forces Programme was closed and incorporated into the domestic services, British audiences for the first time were exposed to innovative programmes such as Radio News Reel, Forces Favourites and Question Time (previously The Brains Trust), as well as a novel five minute review of the daily press.

And of course radio had been used to make all of the major public announcements by prime ministers: Neville Chamberlain declaring war in 1939; Winston Churchill leading a national government from 1940.

And Churchill's wartime radio speeches are now history: 'I have nothing to offer but blood, toil, tears and sweat/Never in the field of human conflict was so much owed by so many to so few/We shall fight on the beaches, we shall fight on the landing grounds, we shall fight in the fields and in the streets. We shall never surrender'. But Churchill's attitude towards the BBC as an organisation was ambivalent. He could see its value as a tool in his aim to be the great communicator, but within weeks of becoming prime minister he was planning a government take-over. He remembered the days of the general strike when the BBC had insisted on carrying reports

Churchill made maximum use of the airwaves

from strikers as well as the government, and concluded that the corporation was not to be trusted. He had also lived through the years since then, when John Reith had continually refused him, as a junior politician, access to the airwaves.

Prime Minister Churchill told Reith that the BBC 'was the enemy within the gate, doing more harm than good'. He was to later describe the BBC as 'one of the major neutrals'. implying that it was not 'one of us'. It was an attitude the corporation would eventually come to expect from every government.

After Reith left the BBC he became head of the Ministry of Information, which in the wartime was responsible for the supervision (censorship) of broadcasting, but Churchill sacked him, for possibly very personal reasons. Luckily, Churchill eventually appointed a successor who was better able to softly hold the ring between diplomacy and independence: Brendan Bracken, owner of the Financial Times. Talk of a government take-over of the BBC was not heard after that.

But after the war it took the BBC over a year, in 1945, to recover from the constant supervision of the Ministry of Information and decide to set up its very first self-sufficient news division. Also, in July, the Light Programme began, with the Third Programme starting two months later.

As the Third Programme was specifically designed for a possibly very worthy but nevertheless minority parallel audience, this could well be seen as the next, fourth, stage in the evolution of BBC radio. With the lessening of governmental leverage on the daily output of the BBC, the process was not unlike the experience of a growing child discovering maturity.

In the seat by then as director general was William Haley, previously of the Manchester Guardian and promoted to the job from being head of editorial content, who was thus perhaps better able than many to re-plan programming.

As he reported: 'Before the war the system was to confront [the listener] with the necessity for pendulum-like leaps. [He] was deliberately plunged from one extreme to the other. The devotees of Berlin (Irving) were suddenly confronted with Bach. Many listeners were won for higher things in this way, but many were irretrievably lost. For the weakness of the process was that so many intolerances were set up.'

So the Haley plan was not to abandon variety and the search of excellence altogether, but to gradually even it out, and to move forward with three parallel programmes: Light, Home and Third: 'Each programme leading onto the other, the listener being induced through the years increasingly to discriminate in favour of the things that are more worth-while. Each programme at any given moment must be ahead of its public, but not so much as to lose their confidence. The listener must be led from good to better by curiosity, liking, and a growth of understanding. As the standards of the education and culture of the community rise so should the programme pyramid rise as a whole.'

Then followed a decade of what many in Britain now call radio's golden days, including ITMA and Mrs Dale's Diary,

Dick Barton, the Goon Show and Children's Hour. The fifth stage of radio evolution was inspired by a competing media, albeit also run by the BBC, the re-launch of television.

Television was invented in the 1920s and in 1930 the BBC tested it, moving on to C as 'one of London-only broadcasts in

1936. But the start of the second world war forced it to a halt. It resumed in 1946, with BBC management insisting on using it as radio with added pictures. As with radio, it took some years of practice to treat it with maturity, to grant it some personal independence and to recognise that it had a character of its own.

Television was the first big challenge to radio

All the same, the novelty of the medium certainly succeeded in stealing audiences from radio, especially when – as with the start of radio – it reported on the big national events, such as the coronation of Elizabeth II in 1953. This attracted an audience of 20 million people, or 56 percent of the British population. Radio could just not compete.

With an audience of this size, it was obvious that the BBC would not be able to maintain a monopoly for long. The fifties were a period in Britain of rapidly rising incomes, so that the call to allow commercial competition, funded by advertising, to BBC television was undeniable. It happened with the birth of the Independent Television Authority in 1955.

The effect of competition on television was to make it much more professional. But the effect of competition on radio – now up against two television channels – was especially dramatic.

BBC radio's average evening audience dropped from nearly 9 million in 1949 to fewer than 3.5 million in 1958 – three quarters of whom had no television receivers, anyway.

The obvious response was to re-examine the comparative nature of radio output, to see in what way it could be made more relevant, to define its particular strengths.

The first conclusion was that there was too much overlap between the three stations, but especially between the Home and the Light. On one hand, it was thought that the Light was sometimes too serious for some listeners – who were deserting again to Radio Luxembourg – while the Third Programme was seen as far too marginal, seldom attracting more than two percent of the total audience. Adjustments were made, some good, some bad.

The audience fell from 9 to 3.5 million in 1958

Stage six of radio evolution came in 1964, with the birth of both pirate radio and BBC2 television. This has been described as BBC radio's lowest ebb. The Third Programme suffered yet another cannibalization and reconstruction, the features department was abandoned (it could not compete with television, so they said) and Children's Hour was killed. (Infanticide?)

Evolution stage seven could also be seen as the start of the resurrection, with three inventions of particular value. The first was stereo broadcasting, tested in 1958 and first applied in the UK in 1966; this gave music in particular a greater physical presence. The second was very high frequency (VHF) and frequency modulation (FM) broadcasting, which together, from 1955 onwards, greatly reduced interference and made broadcasting more geographically specific, thus allowing the birth of genuinely local radio. The third, and arguably the most important, was the transistor, which replaced the bulky radio valve and so made possible smaller receivers. But although it was invented in 1947, it was not in general use in Britain until the 1960s.

The radio landscape had suddenly changed. On one hand it was living in a different frame, made up of television in addition to print. On the other hand, pirate radio had shown how best to exploit the transistor generation, who listened to their new portable radios either while walking around the house or while travelling in cars. Pirates such as Caroline and London opted for continuous background music – for which, of course, they paid no royalties – making no attempt at providing words that would need any special attention. Until then the norm had always been to interleave music with polite conversation, whether relevant or not. The BBC found this ancient tradition for a long time hard to drop.

What was not being realised for quite some while was that the audience for radio was being split between those who listened and those who just heard. The fact that the two were not the same defined a need for different products, which the BBC did not offer.

Most interesting was the estimation that the considerable audience for pirate radio had not been taken from existing audiences, but mainly consisted of a new generation of listeners under thirty.

The BBC responded in 1967 with the launch of (word-light) Radio 1, together with Radios 2, 3 and 4, all with target audiences defined in response to market research. John Reith would have shivered in his grave.

The blueprint for BBC survival was called Broadcasting in the Seventies. The idea of one radio station being all things to all men and women was formally abandoned in favour of four stations being four things to four sides of everyone. This more dispersed, yet inclusive philosophy obviously allowed, within each station, for a greater consistency of mood, subject and mental attitude.

Radio One had already concentrated its output on popular music. Then, in 1970, Radio Two became a network for continuous, middle of the road music, while Radio Three lost many of its speech programmes to Radio Four and instead concentrated on classical music.

Sport continued to be split between Three and Four, but Four considerably increased its output of news and current affairs; the truth had finally hit home that, with the rapid spread of transistor-powered portable receivers, the great edge that BBC radio in particular had over television was its ability to deliver instant information.

All the same, in 1971, the radio-only licence was abandoned in favour of one licence for everything. Radio now had to fight for survival, to prove its worth.

This continual marginalisation seems strange, when considered in a historical context.

Charles Dickens and J K Jerome transformed printed journalism by adopting colloquial English at just the time when labourers were being taught to read. It could equally be said that Radio Four has been transforming broadcast communication by supplying critical information at just the time when professionals were being encouraged to think.

In the early days Prime Minister Stanley Baldwin described BBC radio as 'A milestone along the road to the social betterment of our people' (at the same time as condemning Max Beaverbook's Daily Express for exercising power without responsibility – a phrase he had borrowed from his journalist cousin Rudyard Kipling) while the contemporary Archbishop of Canterbury described BBC radio as 'An essential part of the machinery of civilisation'.

The result is a product of the brute force of monopoly

It is now a truism that the young (and troubled) John Reith had been determined, as the first director general, to use 'the brute force of monopoly' as 'an integrator for democracy' to create 'a more intelligent and enlightened electorate'. Indeed, 'As we conceive it, our responsibility is to carry into the greatest number of homes everything that is best in every department of human knowledge, endeavour or achievement'.

The question asked by Guglielmo Marconi before his death in 1937 'Have I done the world good or have I added a menace?'

was not obviously answered for a long time. My first editor, Malcolm Muggeridge, had replied in a way in 1940 that BBC radio had become 'An image, pure and undefiled, of the times, a mirror held up to nature', but in his later career as a television interviewer he was told by the now much older (and wiser?) John Reith that broadcasting in general had become 'A potential social menace of the first magnitude'. So much for the Reithian tradition.

But (as Gerry Mansell, the first controller of Radio Four said to me recently) that was all such a long time ago.

&

PASSAGE

From there to here

After forty years of Radio Four, changes in society are the main influences on changes in the media. Such as:

Everyone is roughly three times better off financially (there are 400,000 British millionaires, with 900 of them aged under 34 living mainly in London), although the division between rich and poor has widened and most people have more debt; Britain has moved from being an industrial society to a consumer society; pay rates for women are rising faster than for men.

People are living longer (for women to an average of 85 instead of 70) and in the smallest houses in Europe.

Owning your own home in Britain is now normal, while owning another abroad is no longer rare; going abroad on holiday is now common, while visiting Europe is more common than visiting the US, often via the Channel Tunnel.

Three quarters of people who live in London were not born in Britain; London is now the world's most important centre for finance and communications; Britain is the world's biggest exporter of cultural products, including media.

Shops are open all hours; food and clothes cost less; Britain now has more people eating out than any other country in the world; fish and chips have given way to curry as the nation's favourite meal; tea is giving way to coffee and beer to wine as the nation's favourite drinks.

Five times more people are going to university; most university graduates are now women; the most popular university subject is the media.

Informality as a life style is now normal; living together before marriage is now normal; sexual nonconformity is no longer shocking; single parent families have increased threefold.

It is increasingly common to refuse honours from the Queen; the British flag is rarely flown, the national anthem is rarely played; class as a word is now rarely used; people with titles and degrees no longer boast about them

Dressing up has given way to dressing down. Oxbridge accents are seldom heard.

Hardly anyone worships God in public apart from Moslems and a growing number of Christians in London

All institutions have lost public credibility, but parliament more than most.

Most British legislation is created in Brussels; most people do not physically vote; a quarter of the London population do not register to vote; three quarters of the British population do not support the government; only one percent of the population belong to political parties. Civic activism has never been busier.

> Most people have a mobile phone and an awful lot of people (and schools) have computers and log onto the web. Everyone is a great deal better informed about nearly everything.

An increasing proportion of people work from home. One in three also live alone, which is twice as many as forty years ago.

&

The media now

An annual broadcast receiving licence has grown with inflation from £4 for radio only in 1962 to a television only licence of £126 in 2006; spending on communication overall increased nine fold between 1971 and 2006.

There are now as many female editors as male; and there are growing numbers of working - and earning - female readers and listeners.

Most journalists no longer work for just one medium. Those who want a career in media get degrees instead of fetching tea.

Serious newspapers are slowly gaining sales from a low base; popular newspapers are fast losing sales from a high base.

Morning newspapers try to add value with interpretation; all newspapers are more sensational. So is television.

Print media that used to depend mainly on sales income now depend mainly on advertising income; there has been an enormous increase in the number of free and specialist journals; there seems to have been a similar increase in the amount of disposable (poor) journalism in all media.

Reading a daily newspaper is no longer the norm; books are read by commuters as often as newspapers.

> Radio stations and newspapers are moving on-line. Innumerable radio stations now broadcast (mainly music) from all over the place and have long ago abandoned tape recording for digital recording, A handful of television channels has become dozens.

News and the demand for news has moved from 12 hours a day to 24, thus redefining (diluting?) the meaning of news. A stress on what used to be called important public figures has given away to what are called personalities.

> A consolidated mass media, if it ever did exist, clearly no longer does.

The BBC is still one of the most externally admired parts of Britain. People who work for the BBC are still sure they run the world. A few others in the world agree with them.

&

What this means

In the past forty years essential changes in the British way of life have resulted in: more people living alone and working from home, who are more aware of world events and of cultural variations.

People feeling less bound by tradition and more confident of their social position, especially women.

People being less willing to defer to authority and more willing to make their own judgements on a growing number of issues.

People using many more ways of collecting information, but with no great growth in the means of evaluating that information outside of formal education other than through media.

Hence the potential for Radio Four.

&

PRINCIPLES

Defining the public

Let's be honest. The whole country does not listen to Radio Four. At the time of writing, just 9.3 million or 18.7 percent of the British radio public, with an average age of 54, are believed to listen on a regular basis which (although beaten by Radio Two with 26.5 percent and Radio One with 21.4 percent audience share) might be supposed to indicate a strictly minority audience. This, however, would ignore a very important truth. Which is that the influence of Radio Four is very much bigger than its immediate audience, in two ways.

The first is the way in which its output is used as a reference by what can only be described as the decision makers of Britain: politicians, journalists, government officers, academics, lobbyists and so on. My observation and experience is that very few people in these groups, irrespective of their age, do not listen to Radio Four. And some of them go on to develop what they have heard that day into other formats within hours. (Paul Dacre, editor of the Daily Mail: 'I for one would pay the licence fee just for Radio Four.')

The second influence is in the way in which programmes developed for Radio Four are so often redeveloped for television. Drama and comedy (with an especially young audience profile) are obvious examples. After all, new ideas are cheaper to explore - and test - in a radio format.

Apart from this, it is striking to notice that, nationwide, its audience values it more highly than the audience for any other radio station. While in London, Radio Four is also the most popular station, with an audience reach of 23 percent, with Radio Two at 18.6 percent and Heart at 16.2 percent. The share of audience hours listened to is even more impressive, with Radio Four at 16.1 percent, Radio Two at 6.1 percent and Radio Five at 4.8 percent. A look at the economic profile of the city at large gives some explanation for this. London is dominated by service industries, which obviously employ the kind of people who are more likely than others to be well educated in one sense or another, as well as eager to become involved in more than domestic affairs. They seem to need their companionable daily drip feed of cultural cementation.

Previously Radio Four has been described as a middle class station, but I do not personally find the separation of audiences into classes at all useful. Classes are normally described as financial income groups (A, B, C and D) which gives little indication of social awareness. Over half a million Britons earning over £100,000 a year call themselves working class. Meanwhile, some rich people are very ignorant, while poor people can be well informed. Think of monks and academics. They are intellectually aspirant. Knowing, for instance, that income brackets A and B are twice as likely to listen to news on Radio Four as watch news on BBC television must be of some pleasure to radio controllers (and of immense frustration to others, especially if they work in commercial radio), but says little about the likely influence on British public opinion.

At the same time, there is no denying that the British are not very fond of intellectuals and that most of them would fervently deny that they were any such thing. In other countries, people will call themselves doctors or professors as swiftly as they can. Not in Britain, where a ready disclosure of personal assets, intellectual or material, is considered, well, not quite the thing. The first controller of Radio Four, Gerald Mansell, who is as much French as English and who went on to run the World Service, was the first person to draw my attention to this. And considering that he was the one person, as much as any, who developed Radio Four out of the old Home Programme, I am inclined to take his word for it. Hence my suggestion that, even if Britain does not have an intelligentsia, it does have Radio Four. It sets the agenda for thinking people. It sparks debates at work and at home. It opens people's minds.

Britain may not have an intelligentsia, but it does have Radio Four

As another former Radio Four controller, Monica Sims, recently said to me with glee 'I learn so many things'. And this despite the fact that she was also a distinguished editor of Woman's Hour and a major (female) figure in BBC television, and, since then, has been a member of any number of important public bodies. In retirement, glued to what her mother probably would have called a wireless, she is definitely still involved.

But the stark reality is that the audience for BBC radio has, until recently, only slightly and, at times, even reluctantly been recognised by the people who make the programmes. We already know that John Reith - the man credited, rightly or wrongly, with the creation of the Corporation - was distinctly reluctant to give up the role of dictator to one of being a service provider. He believed he knew what was right for everyone.

Post Reith the process of collecting audience reaction became a little more businesslike. And there was a time, in 1967, when the BBC's central Audience Research Department had a permanent staff of 116, with 700 part-time interviewees and 7,500 unpaid volunteers grouped into viewing and listening panels, all ready to provide statistics on audience size, degrees of satisfaction and any other answers to any other questions. As part of this process, some 2,500 members of the public were interviewed every day. The problem then, of course, was knowing what to do with it all. My personal observation is that attitudes vary over the years. The sociologist Tom Burns reported after a year of research in 1973 (published in 1977 in the excellent work 'The BBC: public institution and private world' that, despite all

Tom Burns noted that there was no evidence of people at the top of the BBC even caring what the audience thought

of this information gathering, 'there is no evidence of people at the top of the Corporation knowing, or indeed caring, what the audience makes of the service it receives'. He also considered that 'BBC values depend less on awareness of the public than awareness of senior (and very senior) managers': a problem common to many large organisations. And he then looked beyond number crunching to lament 'the surprising absence, in so exceptionally articulate a working community, of discussion about the social consequencies of broadcasting'.

At the other extreme, in the late nineties an expensively produced document called '100 Tribes' excitedly described the British public as so many demographic groups and insisted that television producers especially considered them when planning programmes. It did not take long to discover, however, that a good programme attracted a good audience equally from every group and that a bad programme did not.

There is no longer a BBC research department in the old mould. Overall audience figures for all broadcasters are now collected centrally by an independent agency (thus avoiding conflicting claims from competing organisations), while the recently emergent marketing departments of the BBC commission other research to order. However, much of this specific research, although publicly funded, is shyly withheld from public view on the grounds of being commercially confidential, which is understandable, I suppose, when BBC television produces programmes which are so similar to commercial stations, but not so understandable when applied to Radio Four. I mean, who can compete with Radio Four?

It is true that competitors have appeared from time to time. I remember presenting the travel report in the morning for the all-talk London Broadcasting Company, which was led for three years by a former editor of the BBC's Today programme, Marshall Stuart. (His morning programme was called AM, which he claimed was being kept by the BBC as an alternative title for Today.) But it became clear that establishing a reputation as strong as the BBC's was not going to happen swiftly, and that important people would not appear on unimportant programmes, so that advertisers were reluctant to pay and investors ran out of money. Radio Four stood proudly alone again. Equally, Channel Four radio, available at the moment only on-line, has claimed that it already competes on-line with Radio Four. But does it? We look at this later in the book.

Uncertainty about the use of media research is not confined to the BBC. Many in journalism will remember the birth of the Sun newspaper out of the Daily Herald. The new owners, who also owned the Daily Mirror, thought that what Britain most needed was a modern daily, produced by modern methods. So, in 1961, a very modern advertising agency (no longer in existence) sponsored a survey to discover exactly which elements of the existing daily press were most valued by their publics. Having identified these elements, they promptly recommended them as the core essential ingredients for the re-titled Herald, The Sun. No sooner said then done. However, nobody seemed to realise at the time that the ingredients that most pleased people about their existing papers were the same reasons why they would not want to switch. Which demonstrated very clearly, of course, not the uselessness of market research, but its misapplication.

Others will remember the Daily Telegraph when it was very much a business belonging to the Berry family. Mr Berry, later Lord Hartwell, decided on the daily news agenda largely as a result of a chat with his wife over breakfast. It just so happened, however, that Lady Hartwell's social antennae and previous evening's dinner guests were very acutely attuned to the mores of middle England, which meant that, despite the anxieties of the staff, such as myself, the Telegraph managed to please most of its public most of the time.

Providers of information have a very good idea of the value of programmes

All the same, quite a lot is publicly known about the audience for Radio Four. Only after moving out of broadcasting into public relations did I discover how keenly these providers of information to journalists and broadcasters studied their targets; also, how acutely aware they are of the value of different programmes.

Useful meat for this can be found in a very readable book produced in 1997 about the Today programme (All our Todays by Paul Donavan), which reported that 24 percent of the network's overall audience then were aged up to 44, which meant of course that 76 percent were older than that.

Listening patterns are also known. Up to half of listeners tune in for up to 8 hours a week, 20 percent for over 21 hours a week and 10 percent for over 30 hours a week.

Public relations people also know that the peak listening period is between 7 and 9.30 am, with a weekly reach from 3.2 to 4 million, peaking at 8.15 am. After the early morning Today programme, it is known that audiences gradually tail away until perking up at lunchtime, to fall and pick up briefly again in the early evening, and then again in the late evening, but to nowhere near the size of audience at the start of the day. Many are away from their homes in the day time, while home workers, which are growing in numbers, having probably tackled mainly manual jobs in the morning with Radio Four as their conversational companion, often opt for more concentrated mental concentration in the afternoon, preferably in the company of unobtrusive music. Then, in the evening, many prefer to relax (and dose?) in front of television. While radio, of course, has as many pictures as you care to imagine. More precisely, the average listener spends 13 hours a week with Radio Four, plus one hour with Radio Three, and one and a half hours each with Radio Five Live or Classic FM. Exactly what proportion of these listening hours consist of hearing as well as listening (or whether they are subject to what has since been called Continuous Partial Attention) is open to question. Of course

The average listener spends thirteen hours a week with Radio Four: no other station competes

there is regional variation. It seems that the very qualities of the network that make it attractive to Londoners apply almost as much to most radio listeners below a line running roughly from The Wirral to The Wash, but not so much above that. Northern Ireland and Scotland have the smallest audiences, but they also have stronger regional programmes, which makes that understandable.

But Britain does not have the only audience. On a recent visit to Spain (where 200,000 Britons now live) I discovered dozens of expatriates with giant aerials, desperately determined to catch Radio Four on long wave. I have another friend in the Philippines who listens on-line and amplifies the outcome out of his windows and down the hill to the nearest village. So who counts all of them?

Apart from counting audience size, there has for long been a use of focus groups, to try to get a better assessment of audience evaluation, but even then the question remains of what to do with the inevitably historic information that this produces. A incredibly detailed book on the BBC at large by Georgina Born called 'Uncertain vision' (produced with a grant of £134,000 from the Economic and Social Research Council) came firmly to the opinion that such work is virtually useless. 'Creativity cannot be enhanced by crude understandings of existing audience tastes' she wrote. And not many would disagree. All the same, the down-loading of programmes has placed another laurel around the head of Radio Four. The process began in 2004 with that year's Reith lecture. At the time of writing the BBC's second most popular programme to download is perhaps the most intellectual analytical programme, at nine on Thursday mornings on Radio Four, In Our Time, with Melvyn Bragg. Normally lasting for forty minutes (the evening repeat is thirty minutes), this dissects an intellectual concept through a panel of complementary experts, with Bragg encouraging clarity. The fact that such a challenging concept attracts an audience so determined to hear it that they go to the trouble to capture it is impressive. The size of its down-load audience, at 251,000 a month, is even more impressive. The question is: what does this mean? Perhaps it means that those most attracted to this kind of programme are also the kind of people most comfortable with new technology. Also that it attracts those with the busiest life style. Perhaps. But above all else it means that measuring and quantifying audiences is going to become much harder than before. So, alongside those who listen on traditional radio receivers there are also those who listen on car radios and through their computers (and overseas), as well as those who listen at any old time to programmes they have down-loaded onto their digital recorders. The traditional attraction of fixed points in the day to draw in the devoted listener seems threatened. So what does mean for an institution?

&

The travails of an institution

The BBC, as an institution, is a kind of tradition. It has been judged the UK's strongest business brand. It is also the biggest media producer in the country, employing 23,000 people in 600 offices in the UK and around the world, with a total income for 2006/7 of £4,415.8m. Its television output attracts 34 percent of the national audience, its radio output 55 percent. It has 240 websites, eight national television channels, ten national radio stations and forty local radio stations.

It is globally seen as the guardian of the English language and the British way of life, as well as the champion of truth and fair play. (Everyone's been stuck in a corner at a party with a complete stranger holding you to account for every failure of your particular profession, but only people who work for Radio Four, I swear, are also held to account for safeguarding the sanctity of the English language. As if there were only one form of English.)

Tradition, of course, can be both a blessing and a handicap. For many years I thought it was the greatest curse that Britons had to bear, especially because 'We don't do things that way' has nearly always been the reaction of editors to journalists who try to move the debate forward and move the format forward. I had to go to Canada to produce public service radio that I thought was fit for the modern world. I did not change that sense of irritation until about ten years ago, when I found myself sitting next to Wolf Olins, the presentational genius, at an annual meeting of the British Council when the director announced that their objective for the next year would be to present Britain abroad as the true seat of modernity and progress, if only because so many inventions had been British. 'Rubbish' shouted Olins, quivering in his tweed suit, 'If the USA is already seen as the seat of invention, rightly or wrongly, we would be mad to fight that and not provide the world with what they expect of us, which is quality and tradition. It is our greatest asset.'

The flavour of that objective was caught exactly by Humphrey Carpenter's book on the Third Programme and Radio Three in its title The envy of the World. The book also, inevitably, includes many references to Radio Four, as the two stations have inter-related in different ways for a number of years.

The most important impression I got from Carpenter's work was that the champion of the BBC and its cultural standards should not be seen as John Reith, but William Haley. BBC radio before Haley in the 1930's had great difficulty providing anything not middlebrow. The novelist Evelyn Waugh, albeit being the greatest snob of all time, nevertheless spoke for many with aspirations when he dismissed the life style of those who 'lived in the radio-ridden villas of the Sussex coast'. While the more serious novelist Harold Nicholson, then a governor of the BBC, wrote that 'an oily unctuous coating of compromise descended upon the presentation of the more difficult items.' But when Reith had left the BBC he was succeeded by F W Ogilvie, whom Humphrey Carpenter describes as being unable to make decisions and sticking to them, which led to his forced retirement four years later. Ogilvie was then succeeded, in an excess of compromise, by two joint director generals, who proved no better.

Luckily, Brendan Bracken, the founder of the FT and then minister for information, insisted to the governors that something substantially different needed to be done, which resulted in the journalist William Haley - formerly a director of The Manchester Guardian and later editor of The Times - being appointed to the new post of editor in chief in 1943.

William Hayley's influence on the BBC seems to have been overlooked

Haley (sometimes known as the man with two glass eyes because of his riveting gaze) was an odd ball in having had no university education, but who had nevertheless become managing director of the Manchester Guardian through sheer hard work and self-education. In 1944 he became director general. He was nothing if not decisive. 'I think one of the great things in life is not to be afraid of making mistakes. God knows one's made hundreds.' In any case, Haley brought about the birth of the Third Programme after two years in post, in 1946, which, at least in principle, enabled what might be called more aspirational broadcasts to be offered without apology.

But the core of Haley's motivation was described by Carpenter in a record that had been kept by a new South African entrant to the BBC, Etienne Amyot, who arrived after wartime service in Psychological Warfare. Amyot remembered a number of conversations in which Haley stressed the immense reputation that the BBC had gained around the world, not for propaganda, but for telling the truth, which created a need to find a way of extending that into peacetime, so that 'people can become not more educated, but more enlightened. He wanted the BBC to have a great civilising influence.'

For me this puts Haley in the central position of having championed the evolved BBC we know, rather more than the narrowly fixed (and rather hypocritical) strictures of Reithism.

Nevertheless, conventions are conventions, and it has always struck me that working for the BBC was not dissimilar to working for a government department. Men in grey suits have for long been dominant. Security clearance was commonly enforced. Oxbridge attitudes – and, for many years, accents – were equally the norm. Despite having previously worked for The Times, The Telegraph, the Financial Times and The Economist, my own foray into Radio Four programmes was very much eased by having learnt the trade at BBC Radio London, which was oddly

A Christmas tree on your personnel file was an ominous sign

seen, by BBC standards, as having been at the forefront of the newly discovered youth culture.

This was, of course, simply a sign of the illogical insecurity found in all large organisations. Other signs included the realisation that I was writing, at that time, for relatively learned journals such as New Society, and so, naturally, I was assumed to have also become a social expert. The reverse was really the truth. My articles in New Society were actually side-products of reports for the BBC. As a freelance, I was working for a number of programmes. But who can refuse a compliment, especially when it includes a commission and a cheque?

Tom Burn's study of the BBC in 1977, mentioned earlier, gave him a similar impression. He noticed how very similar the production staff were in their backgrounds. He asked them whether they intentionally recruited from their own backgrounds. They often hesitated before answering, but usually admitted that yes, they did. If nothing else, it is remarkable how the family name of Dimbleby occurs so often. While the close involvement of the security services in hiring and firing in the BBC has been notable for years; seeing a symbolic Christmas tree drawn on their personnel file was a sign enough for some that their prospects were limited.

Some people fit in better than others. A very comfortable but popular co-presenter of the early Today programme, John Timpson, admitted that while he sometimes regretted not being paid as well as some of his freelance colleagues 'There was considerable prestige in being on the staff of the BBC. You really felt you were somebody. It was second only to the House of Commons as the best club in town, a nice feeling to be part of the establishment and I suppose I became a typical establishment figure'. He certainly did. He was very proud to be invited to Buckingham Palace and 10 Downing Street.

Another co-presenter of the Today programme from 1982 to 1993 was Peter Hobday, who, although extremely popular, was a freelance and thus 'allowed to go' with absolutely no fanfare, or even a modest thanks. It is not surprising then, in retrospect, if his memory of the BBC institution was slightly different to Timpson's. He said of the more recent programme editors that 'there was a growing tendency to do what their masters wanted and listen to the marketing men. The desire to make programmes took second place for a BBC career. The sooner they could get off the journalism, the better'.

This BBC convention for conventionalism was stressed in an excellent study of contemporary journalism, Truth or Dare? by Ian Hargreaves, who had been not only director of news and current affairs for the BBC, but also deputy editor of the FT, editor of The Independent and editor of the New Statesman: 'You would not want to live only with journalism produced by an institution like the BBC: it would be too cautious, too dull.'

Although this conformity is no longer as strong as before (racial minorities are now less minor and recruiting from competing media more common) it explains a BBC faith in itself as a firmly-fixed part of the British way of life. And the near-global omnipresence of the BBC, in its many forms (World Service, on-line, etc) helps to reinforce this.

Not only journalists, but also government officers in every country I have visited have been swift to refer to the BBC as the paragon of virtue when it comes, say, to government and media relations. It is hard at times to disillusion them by pointing out that the BBC's battle with the British government has always been a long-running and expensive process. 'Ah, yes, but for us life is harder' is how they respond. Which is true.

Arguably, however, even in Britain it is also harder for BBC people who work in radio. The two source books I have already referred to, excellent as they are, each deal with the BBC and its 27,000 staff as a single entity, mainly concerned with television and with radio referred to only in asides. Equally, a search of any newspaper will give you reams of information about television programmes, coming or gone, but only the dear old Radio Times has anything approaching proper radio programme listings. Meanwhile, critical coverage of radio output is generally nearly invisible. And within the BBC itself the budget for radio has to be the subject of internal negotiation between managers, with no input of opinion offered to the audience.

Traditional literature treats the BBC as an exclusively television broadcaster

None of which reflects the importance of radio. And certainly not of Radio Four - which, after all, has a bigger audience than any television channel apart from BBC1.

And Radio Four is a serious business. For instance, in 2006 it spent £71.4m in producing 7,960 hours of programming - from 5.35 am to 1 am, seven days a week - at an average hourly cost of £11,500. Of that, 2,499 hours were described as current affairs and factual and 2,334 hours as news and weather. Its total audience share is bigger than any other radio network with the exception of BBC Radios One and Two and bigger than any BBC television audience with the exception of BBC One. All of which makes the lack of attention by print media of radio, and of Radio Four in particular, all the more remarkable.

Remembering Radio Four in the annual budget was seen as a charitable act

The BBC annual report for 2005 declared that during the government's public negotiation on renewing the BBC charter 'there has been general agreement that if the BBC did not broadcast [Radio Four] would not exist, because it would not be financially viable as a commercial operation.' Which makes it sounds almost like a charitable operation. But what it did not say was that, if the BBC did not broadcast Radio Four, the BBC itself may not be able to exist, at least in its present form, as Radio Four clearly delivers, in my view, the bulk of what are called the BBC's public service obligations, at an annual cost of £71.4 million, which represents a 2.2 percent share of total broadcast expenditure.

But running the BBC has also been similar to running a government department, insofar as it was common to see subtle (and sometimes not so subtle) manoeuvring behind the scenes by section heads (otherwise known as barons), each determined to seize political leadership, together with a bigger budget. And that, in my view, has had particularly damaging consequencies for Radio Four. It has been said that the maximum number of people who can relate to a manager on a regular basis is one hundred. Which, if true, makes it obvious that managers at a lower level than director general have to play a significant part in running the BBC. Which will lead to competition.

There is a wealth of material (evidence, gossip) about the performance and personalities of Radio Four controllers over the years, for instance: the becalming Gerry Mansell, the coruscating Tony Whitby, the dour Ian McIntyre, the erudite Alasdair Milne, all of whom helped to shape Radio Four, but always with limited outcomes.

Not until Sir Christopher Bland became BBC chairman did the old feuds between the divisional barons end. Before that, it was common practice, for instance, for the news bulletin section of the Today programme to totally ignore the rest of the programme, which led to a lot of confusion for the audience. Duplication of subjects were common, as well as conflicting treatment. Neither baron would compromise; their territory was sacred.

But possibly the greatest change to working practices within the institution known as Radio Four was the introduction of independent production in 1994. Yet again, this process was introduced to radio, and mainly to Radio Four, years after it had happened on television. Of course television involves the biggest budgets but, in terms of social outcome, it could have been seen as at least as urgent a move for radio. All the same, the use of the phrase independent has to be used with caution. Some ten percent of Radio Four output is currently classified as independent (as apposed to 25 percent of BBC television production), meaning that it comes from one or more of the two dozen external organisations who bid for the business.

Inevitably, perhaps, these companies are largely staffed by former BBC producers, working with the benefit of understanding acceptable norms. Writing as someone who made one of the first independent radio programmes (albeit for commercial radio in the 1980s) I would, of course, question whether the use of former BBC staff is the best way of encouraging cultural, as apposed to financial, independence.

&

What is public service?

So there's this phrase: public service broadcasting, within which Radio Four is said to be a dominant part. The Corporation in certainly fond of the phrase, using it whenever possible as a prefix to the word broadcasting whenever possible, which is often. What does it mean? I don't know. Personally I suspect it means as much as motherhood and apple pie. Everyone says they are in favour of it, but, of course, once it comes to defining the recipe for perfect motherhood and perfect apple pie there are problems.

There is a sort of mutual conspiracy here. When politicians anywhere in the world seek to ensure that a dominant broadcaster does not abuse its near monopoly on the supply of information they look for broad phrases that indicate a suitable set of values. Sometimes they go into detail. Such as the proportion of airtime given, say, to news. Or, more generally, to public information. And who would argue with that?

Yes, but then try defining, precisely, on an individual basis, what qualifies as news and public information and, once again, you will immediately fall into a morass of dispute involving personal values and taste. Is a footballer's broken ankle as important as a ministerial announcement? Etcetera.

However, the obvious reason for broadcasters being only too happy to claim that they are providing a public service is because of the kudos. It is an obvious competitive advantage. It suggests a right to privileges not granted to competitors. So references to what is called PSB are made at frequent intervals.

For instance, there are thousands of euros of taxpayers money spent each year on grand international conferences debating PSB - or promoting PSB, as the organisers would say. The Council of Europe in Strasbourg is strong on this. Their role in promoting democracy includes a commitment to free media. Free of political interference, that means. The fact remains, however, that in real life this commitment is largely ignored. Which is bound to be the case, I suppose, when politicians are being asked to police themselves.

The BBC is a public service content carrier, isn't it?

Hence, in Britain, we have had a supposedly independent board of governors appointed to supervise the BBC nevertheless being (shall we say?) reformed by government pressure. It could be argued that this is small beer when compared with political interference with public broadcasters in other European countries. It could also be argued that, for as long as the BBC is held up to the rest of the world as a standard of excellence, it is very much big beer.

More recently, the BBC has tried to back out of its role as a public service broadcaster and back into a role as a broadcaster carrying public service content. If you find it hard to spot the difference here,

Which brings us onto another aspect of public service: opinion. It could be said that no part of the presentation of information can be free of values. The mere selection of one fact and the deletion of another is a process of personal judgement. This kind of debate employs a lot of time within the BBC. Rules are forever being rewritten in an attempt to make the process of production consistent to a certain set of values, only to show that those values, over time, have changed.

Meanwhile, the rulebook grows. (If you have exhausted the magic of the proposed EU constitutional treaty you could try switching to the BBC's Editorial Guidelines. Many happy hours are guaranteed. Or not. Or else you could more deftly memorise just one sentence from a report into the BBC by a body called The Pilkington Committee in which they suggested that 'Good broadcasting is a practice, not a prescription'.)

A typical conundrum within the public service concept on Radio Four, and elsewhere, besets the perceived need for balance. This is less frenetic than it used to be. It has long been thought desirable that a left-wing point of view ought to be balanced, within the same report, with a right-wing view. Or an argument in favour of an issue aught to be balanced by one that opposes it. This sounds fine in principle, but is less easy in real life. There are usually, obviously, more than left and right extremes in politics. More recently it could be argued that there no extremes at all. And there are seldom only two points of view on any issue. All the same, the limited attentiveness of any radio audience means that any subject has to have a maximum time designated to it, so something has to go. Deciding what goes in and out is central to the job of journalism.

(Possibly the most unique of magazines in New York was called Overmatter, which simply culled all the material kept out of mainstream newspapers; it was sometime libellous, but fascinating. In Britain we have Private Eye.)

Nowadays in the BBC it is thought acceptable to ensure a range of views over a period of time and not especially within a single programme. This creates more work for somebody, but I don't suppose they mind.

Minority interests will always be a problem for some, if not for everyone

The other aspect of what is thought of as PSB is ensuring a voice for minorities, even if it means creating a space at a time when the audience is already minor. I remember a happy year reporting for a Radio Three programme called 'The positive World', which went out so late at night, and at the weekend, that the audience was said to be too small to be measurable. The ethical objective was to show that not all news has to be bad news but, of course, not many were able to witness this. From my point of view it took me to many places around the world I could not have otherwise visited. Which was positive enough, I thought. Another way of serving minorities is to give them employment.

For a few years the BBC followed a publicly conspicuous policy of positive discrimination in favour of employing journalists from racial minorities, which obviously produced a deal of resentment from other members of staff who thought they were being passed over by people less skilled or talented. It also produced a deal of discomfort in those who were promoted in this way.

Knowing that you are being given a job mainly because of the colour of your skin, rather than your innate ability, does little for your confidence. I realised this when I produced a nationally comparative report for the Council of Europe, and also because I knew many victims. But the political drive was strong in those days for the BBC to be seen to be an equal employer in every way. But 'seen' is the word to stress here. Racial minorities in television are common. They are still very rare in radio.

&

News as an addiction

First, it is important to understand that news is a part of Radio Four, but not of Radio Four: it is provided to the station by a central newsgathering unit that serves the whole of the BBC at a total annual cost of £141.3m. A significant result of this is that the radio news department makes the Today programme for Radio Four, as well as the World at One, PM, the World Tonight, Broadcasting House and the World this Weekend

That said, the total news output of the BBC tends to be more highly prized, in my opinion, by non-Brits than Brits. Even though a British survey in 2005 showed BBC radio news to be valued three times more highly than news on commercial stations.

But not until you've spent time in another country are you likely to grasp the full international contrast. And then, as so many programmes on Radio Four relate in some way to issues in the news, in a way quite unlike any other network, it is fair to say that news provides an almost essential backbone to it.

Of course, all broadcasters in every country give regular space to what they call news, but in terms of relevance and reliability it seldom compares in value. On the other hand, all news can also be addictive. Which is why broadcasters are always keen to have as much of it as they can, at least in terms of frequency. Short, strong and regular injections; that is the pattern most preferred. Even if the main news story remains the same for twenty four hours. Just dig the needle in. This is why, in portentous moments, programme makers refer to news as the essence of the BBC. It may be a drug, but it's quality.

(Personally, when I worked on the news desk and had to present the same lead story every half hour, I long had this fantasy of a bulletin that said: so sorry, there is no news today. The probable truth that few people listen to radio all day long made it no less tedious for me.)

Nevertheless, a major advantage of radio news, at least in principle, is that it can be delivered more speedily than any other form of news. If necessary, a mobile phone will get a reporters' voice straight onto a live news programme, while television crews, even with miniature cameras, may struggle to focus on a picture. And any electronic means of reporting will, of course, beat a print medium by hours, even days. So that makes radio king, in my view.

One curious side effect of this is when newspapers are being quoted. This tradition within the BBC sprung from an early governmental insistence that BBC people should not comment on the news. So quoting the views of other media was a convenient way around this. And the national newspapers have been glad to assist, going to enormous trouble to see that early copies of editions are delivered to the studios. The motivation of their publishers is all too clear: as the audience for Radio Four is many times bigger than their own circulations, even bigger than them all put together, the publicity could be enormously useful in helping to sell extra copies. The curiosity comes when it is so often obvious that the papers are simply following stories from the previous day on Radio Four - and especially when some aspect of the story was actually developed by Radio Four. So who is promoting whom?

Thankfully, the rule about comment on the news has now been relaxed, or at least re-interpreted. The process of putting events into context is now seen as a form of comment which is, at least on the face of it, impartial. Indeed, much of the public would be lost without it. And this, again, is where Radio Four truly comes into its own: putting everything into context. Old news, new news, whatever.

News is whatever I say it is or what somebody does not want you to know

Not many years ago there were never-ending and tortuous attempts to add value and interpretation (if not comment) to current events by wheeling in journalists from other media, most of whom had limited ability to speak with clarity and some of whom were extremely doubtful in terms of reliability. Then the decision was made to recruit in-house experts on every essential subject, if necessary from print media, and this made an enormous difference to the quality of reporting. If nothing else, it made public spokesmen much more willing to be interviewed, as the interviewer was much more likely to have a good grasp of the subject. There are few more negative moments for an interviewee (and the public) than rebuffing banal questions.

There have been many deft/daft definitions of the meaning of news, from 'News is something that somebody does not want you to know' to 'News is whatever I say it is'. Both might be true, but I think it best for the moment to put that particular decision to one side. The creation of the commodity is not so obvious.

It might be thought that journalists spent most of their time roaming the world, talking to people that matter, and thus collecting essential items of topicality and interest. Not so. Most journalists (increasingly) seldom leave their desks. So they use their telephones and computers and what is wrong with that?

What is wrong with that is that they become dependent on whatever other people chose to tell them or send them, qualified mainly by the ability to check this information by direct contact with alternative sources, either human or written.

What is further wrong with that, at least potentially, is that, no matter how you may test the original information against information from others, you are still being driven by other people's news agendas. This includes agendas set into motion by other journalists; agendas possibly also created as a result of initiatives taken by others. So who are these others?

In theory, any member of the public. In practice, mainly those who are sufficiently well organised and sufficiently well financed to establish a method and machinery to put a message across. For the sake of convenience, I will call them spokesmen.

Communicating with the public is of course the main purpose of most of these messages, whether they come from governments, businesses or pressure groups, but the media is the most efficient means so far of being able to reach that public.

This is not to deny that, physically, there are many other ways of communicating with the public, but the reality is that messages delivered through some kind of critical filter, meaning journalists, are known to be the most acceptable. Direct communication of any kind is often received with reserve and suspicion, especially if delivered in the language of publicity and advertising.

However much the motivation of print or broadcast journalists may be suspect, they are still preferred for the delivery of messages coming from others. This is why the public relations business is generally so healthy. Promoting the indirect delivery of messages in this way is cheaper than advertising and, when it works, more effective.

For five years I edited and published a quarterly review of communicating policy through media called Spokesman and was always amazed at the greater interest in the subject as a discipline in other countries than in Britain. It has been ethically more acceptable to (be seen to) promote your own interests in the US than in Britain, but the almost total neglect of the process here has lead very obviously to some enormous failures in the delivery of public policy. Being right is useless unless others also accept that you are right; so convincing them of that is essential.

In Britain the managed process of effective communication did not take hold, in government, until the election of the Labour government in 1997. If it has faltered since then it has been because the style of delivery became distorted. The messenger, in the form of the Prime Minister's spokesman, eventually became the message, simply because the natural competition between journalists and spokesmen was allowed to get out of hand.

'Spin' is a label for somebody else's sense of values

Journalists will always bad mouth spokesmen, partly because they resent being dependent on them, partly because they want to avoid admitting they are. Hence journalists will scorn spokesmen who try to do their work in a systematic way on the grounds that the spokesmen are trying to be devious rather than efficient. Equally journalists will bad mouth other journalists, because they are in competition with them as well. Print journalists will slur broadcast journalists, national journalists will slag off local journalists, and so on. None of this is worth bothering about.

Much more important is the ability of journalists to deliver a fair and balanced account of any event or situation to their publics. And even more important is their ability to present the right sort of news to the right sort of public. Insofar as all journalists monitor/compete with the work of other journalists, there are inevitably fashions in news. Diverting that process away from traditional formats, influencing fashion, is an enormously important function, at least for journalists.

For instance, everyone now knows about global warming. But thirty years ago, when scientists were first talking about it, there was hardly a whisper in the national media. Equally thirty years ago, several thousand people in the US knew about AIDS, but it took at least ten years to be seriously considered in the UK. And so on. This was not the result of a positive decision to not cover these issues by British journalists, but simply the lack of any efficient process of ensuring that they knew about them.

On the other hand, there has seldom been a day when we failed to hear about the troubles of Israel, certainly when compared with the troubles of Palestine. And this has nothing to do with the relative strengths of the two arguments, but a lot to do with the provision of a process whereby the view of one side was made more readily available to journalists, while the other was not.

So, are journalists to blame for this? Largely, yes. If only because the majority of editors are nervous of running stories that are not being used by other media. Being different requires much bravery. On the other hand, there is nothing to stop responsible groups of individuals from employing professional communicators to ensure that journalists do hear their messages.

However, most spokesmen would prefer to present their messages as simply a variation on a current issue; this makes attracting the attention of lazy reporters and conservative editors that much easier and more likely to succeed. Hence, once an editor makes it known that he plans to commission regular reports on a subject such as the environment, everyone in the public relations business will immediately look for ways of presenting everything they are paid to promote within an environmental context. Newsrooms will be awash with press handouts. Computers will bulge with facts, pictures, announcements and assertions. Pages and airtime will be filled in minutes. But will the public be any the wiser?

The reluctance of editors to determine their own agenda is their problem

To help illustrate the options available in the definition of news it could be useful to consider news management. This is a phrase used in the business of public relations that journalists love to hate but which they usually do little to prevent. In my view, news management is when journalists allow themselves to be managed.

For instance, the simple selection of topics for a news bulletin and the order in which they are presented is either motivated by a desire for conformity (what other news media are likely to do) or the result of deliberate non-conformity (what others are not expected to do). In practice, the variation in each theme depends partly on where the editors see their target audience and partly on how brave/rash they are in wanting to be different. Bearing in mind that every editor sees himself as competing with other media, he just cannot ignore them, any more than his public can. Hence lobbyists who need to get their messages used by news media, or any media, bear these factors in mind and use them to their advantage.

To illustrate that: when working in public relations I once needed to promote a financial product of relevance mainly to readers of the Financial Times, but, being in conservative mode at that time, they showed no interest. The answer was to give the story to the usually neglected financial reporters on The Independent, although we knew the paper to have very few readers in our target audience. The immediate response, the next day, was that the Financial Times realised that they had been out-scooped on a financial story by The Independent, so published a follow-up. There is little doubt in my mind that this was an example of news management in which the journalists concerned had willingly taken part. It was not my decision, but theirs.

The enormous growth of lobbyists has certainly cast doubt on a lot of information

Equally, when I helped to promote the launch of a new merchant bank, the first such launch since the second world war, it was clear to me that very few news editors - who control the news agenda - have a clear idea of what any bank does, quite apart from the specialist activities of a merchant bank, so that pre-announcing such an event was not likely to inspire a great deal of interest or anticipation. The solution was to commission a respected financial journalist to compose a background brief on the importance to Britain of specialist banking that even the most reactionary of news editors could appreciate and to attach that to the press invitation to the launch. The result was blanket coverage on the front page of every national newspaper and an item on every broadcast news programme. Again, the response of journalists was their own decision.

Often it is hard for journalists to know who they are talking to, which is where specialist knowledge is so important. Lately there has been a trend to establish foundations, or publications, or think tanks, or charities, with worthy sounding titles, which are nevertheless paid for by interested parties with very definite stories to tell. For instance, it took many years for the truth to come out that Encounter, an influential monthly magazine of opinion in Britain, had been entirely funded by the CIA.

Over the same period, in the world of agriculture, the dominance of just two pressure groups, the National Union of Farmers and the Soil Association, has now been succeeded by some six hundred pressure groups, many of which will act in concert, some openly, say through the Countryside Alliance, some less so. It is obvious that weary news editors need to be wary.

Some journalists have been complicit in helping those 'on the other side' to put their messages across. Specifically, well known presenters have for many years made an additional living by conducting courses for businessmen and others on how to be interviewed. It had long been a normal form of 'retirement' for television presenters such as Cliff Michelmore and Michael Barrett, but more recently they were joined by presenters from Radio Four's Today programme such as Peter Hobday, Sue McGregor and John Humphreys.

Although most presenters are engaged on freelance contracts, the BBC insisted in 1995 that batting on both sides at once, so to speak, had to come to an end. Personally I believe that this is best for everyone, as there was nothing I feared more as a radio reporter than trying to record an interview with someone who had obviously been 'trained'. The outcome was nearly always a lot of time wasted as they went through an unconvincing prepared routine, which I would ignore, then start the interview again.

The importance of setting the news agenda is not only of importance to what are called news programmes. Every journalistic output, every Radio Four programme, is subject to the influence of external opinion, which changes from day to day. To this extent, all output is news.

Ways of influencing the agenda are many. The critical factor to remember is that all information belongs to its originators until they chose to offer it to others, such as journalists. This they can do at any time and in any place of their choice. Great care is taken now in government, for instance, to co-ordinate press information in order to avoid competition or clashes between departments.

There is a big business in future planning, where agencies keep lists of who plans to say what and when, so that others, in any kind of activity, can do their best not to clash. There is obviously a limit to how many stories can be used on any day, especially in the same area of business. On the other hand, some journalists will do their best to work around those carefully-paid plans, especially if they have personal contacts inside of the organisation. And on yet another hand, spokesmen will sometimes help selected journalists to do this, by feeding them information ahead of all the others. This is normally called a leak, although it could just as well be called a tap.

Spokesmen deliberately provide reporters with what are called leaks, although they could just as well be called taps

Back in Radio Four, programme divisions have moved in a variety of ways over the years, partly because the subjects change in nature, partly because those in charge of them differ in ability, but the division closest to news has usually been called current affairs. For the purposes of this book, this is where I group the Today programme, the World at One, PM, etc. After that I would group the purely political programmes, such as Today in Parliament and The Week in Westminster. Anything beyond that, such as the analytical or conversational programmes, do not sound like current affairs to me. Which raises an interesting point. Which is the domination of news by politics.

&

The political masters

Politicians do not run the world, of course, but an observer from outer space listening to Radio Four, or following any other news media in Britain today, might think that they did. Which is what I personally believe to be at the core of what is now commonly accepted to be an ever increasing problem in public life, for politicians, the media and the public: a lack of involvement in politics. And for this I blame the media. But the media also suffers.

When I first worked in radio as a reporter an interview with a politician was a rarity. It was extremely hard to drag them away from Parliament. When you did it was just across the road, into a small, self-operating studio, which had to be unlocked with a key taken from a hook in Broadcasting House and carried down Regent Street. At the end of the interview you would lock up the studio and take the key back, until it was needed again, perhaps the next day, perhaps not.

Nowadays there is a substantial building a little further away from Parliament containing dozens of television and radio studios and which is packed for much of the day with politicians (rather more than you'll find in Parliament) hoping to be interviewed. And they often succeed. There are hundreds of broadcast interviews taking place every day.

The reason for this is obvious. Politicians clearly now believe that they can reach their public, any public, more effectively through direct involvement with the media than by attending debates in Parliament. And the broadcast media have an obviously bigger audience than any other. And Radio Four, most believe, has the most influential audience.

Inevitably, however, the media has an effect on the message. An effective politician nowadays needs to look good (tidy) on television and sound good (friendly) on radio. Alongside this, the oratorical form of presentation which suits a debating chamber, where politicians also appear, in a studio seems ridiculous. All of a sudden, the same politicians who are trying to forge a trusting relationship with their publics seem two-faced, hypocritical.

'When a bulletin starts with a political announcement I know there is no news'

But that is only a slight reason for this growing disillusionment. Another, more important, I suggest, is the institutional decision to exploit the services of the media, by national governments and political parties, employing a virtual regiment of media relations specialists whose job it is to encourage politicians to produce media friendly products. (This does not apply to local government, which generally tries to avoid the media.) The result of this is a constant stream of information and interview material, carefully rationed over a given time, sufficient to fill all the space available in every broadcast outlet.

One potential result of that is to create the impression, through the media, that life in Britain is totally dependent on laws for its heartbeat; implying that those who simply work, creating wealth, supplying services, merely making Britain great, will never make the grade. And this is made real by a compliant media that allows that potential realisation, which includes, of course, Radio Four. When 'important' statements from 'important' people are instantly available at any time, why bother to look any further? This is just what the monstrous news machine needs. No sweat. Let's go for lunch.

The outcome of that is a constant implication that the world will change within minutes of a bulletin; the usual reality is that nothing changes; the result is disillusion. As Tom Burns had already observed in his book 'The BBC' in 1977, based on careful comparative research since the 1950s, 'There has been what seems an almost compulsive drive to politicise almost every aspect of human affairs'. It is much the same now. As a friend of mine says 'When a news bulletin starts with a statement from a politician, I know there is no news.'

This domination of news by politics - or government - is mainly the result of a much tighter organisation of information in recent years by governments of all colours. A daily meeting in Downing Street of departmental heads of government information ensures a regular flow of stories to the media without overlap. Moreover, the stories with the greatest potential tend not to go first to the subject specialists - who may, after all, ask difficult questions - but to the political reporters in parliament, who are always grateful to demonstrate how essential they are and who, quite incidentally of course, seldom have the time or ability to handle the story with any degree of discretion. But the public are not so foolish. With any subject of which they have knowledge, they immediately read between the lines. So, yet more disillusion.

The combined result of all these faults is an increasing rejection of politicians. It seems that our democratic rights have been handed over to empty vessels, meekly following the media herd. The speed and immediacy of broadcast journalism is setting the agenda for representatives who in fact represent just a mere minority, the minority who vote. If you add to that the uncertain relationship in Britain of national to local government, as well as to the European Commission (where most laws are made), then the futility strikes home.

In short, the media has become part of the process of over-valuing Westminster politicians; it is inevitable, then, that the reporting of their politics will also lose appeal.

Of course, the style of political interviewing has substantially shifted over time. Deference has faded from view. Familiarity is now the rule. But most politicians have come to accept this and have spent a lot of time and money in discovering how to exploit it. The biggest remaining problem for them, as they see it, is to restore the balance of power between them and the troublesome media; to influence, ideally to set, the agenda for news from day to day, while they talk disparagingly of consumer politics without seeing it as a plus.

It is interesting in this respect to remember that the phrase Fourth Estate came to be given to the British press in the 18th century when it assumed the essential role in society previously held, but abandoned, by parliament as a counter to the power of the Crown, the Church and government. So the logic of politicians expecting parity with journalists is not immediately clear.

One of the most determined if not very popular BBC director generals, John Birt, amazed his colleagues in 1995 by telling them that 'democratically elected politicians have a higher claim to speak for the people than journalists', thus disowning the Fourth Estate, it seems. No wonder he wasn't popular.

Exactly what is the power of the media?

In the world of politics and media, conspiracy theories abound. Eminent academics wonder whether journalists should share the same freedom of expression as other people 'considering the power they have'. What power? It has never been defined.

A best selling book for many years carried the title 'Power without responsibility: the press and broadcasting in Britain', while also failing to define that power or that lack of responsibility; some would say that satisfying a constantly paying public is the only responsibility necessary.

Equally the concentration of media companies into the hands of ever fewer companies has been declared to limit access to information, while (1) ignoring the shrinking markets for such inevitably weakened products, (2) confusing reach with influence, and (3) ignoring the much faster growth of alternative media, usually with no corporate involvement. This all reflects earlier academic scare stories about the power of the mass media, which as far as I can tell never existed, either in terms of power or in terms of mass. Who appoints such academics?

On the other hand, there is a case for considering the responsibility of media in setting the conversational agenda. And not just whether they should, but whether they do, and how?

It is interesting to talk to a press attaché at a London embassy and to realise how much their jobs depend largely on delivering a daily analysis to their national governments on the opinion columns in British national dailies. They seem to seldom realise that only a very few people read these columns in Britain and that nobody, as far as I can tell, is ever influenced by them. If they have any influence on policy at all, it surely could never compare with that of an interview on Newsnight or Today. But what this does stress is the different approach to media in different countries.

Equally, spokesmen in the European Commission anguish about the counter-productive effects of anti-European headlines in papers such as The Sun, without apparently realising that people read the Sun not for information, but for fun. And then there is the question about media affecting policy. Nik Gowing, a BBC television presenter, took advantage of a scholarship at Harvard to spend a year defining the influence of media on policy-making during the first Gulf War, which had been described both by soldiers and politicians as having been a serious problem. He interviewed at length over a hundred policy makers involved in the war, in Paris, Washington and London and produced no evidence at all for the assumption. Talk, quite clearly, is not the same as action and may not even lead to it.

But the Achilles heel of the BBC is surely its dependency on politicians, on parliament, to continually renew its charter and to guarantee its licence fee. On the other hand, the niggling itch for national politicians is the unspoken knowledge that the principle reason for state control has long since passed away. With a limited band width at a time of war, there was clearly a need for intervention.

Those times have now long gone. Satellites now girdle the world. While anyone using the world wide web can effectively be their own broadcaster, even if in an amateur way, so that any attempt to control such growth is transparently absurd.

But, with a guaranteed income, will the Beeb admit this? That is equally absurd.

&

The moving context

No media is an island, as you might say, while the importance of London in the world of communication is impressive. Whether London is the capital of the communication world is, I suppose, disputable, but I am not aware of any competitors. So, if my assertion of the influence of Radio Four on the life of Britain is also accepted, this context only stresses that.

Let me spell it out. First, there is the history which created the structure. As part of building the British empire (yes, it had to come in somewhere), alongside of the emerging industrial revolution, an immense web around the world was created of telephonic communication, radiating from London. Each time a new link was made, it was made with London. Hence, eventually, countries next to each other in, say, Africa, depended entirely on London to communicate with each other.

This physical structure also, inevitably, created an intellectual structure, based on access to information, techniques and languages, again dominated by London. But now that this early telephonic structure has been made largely redundant by advances in other forms of physical communication, with satellites and so on, the intellectual structure still remains. Moreover, over the years it has accumulated a multiplicity of complementary skills, contributed by specialists from dozens of countries, each with an especial contribution to make. Hence you will find in London today a vast and inter-related community of communication specialists, using many languages and with expertise on every possible form of media, each of which relates to each other.

One outcome of this is, for instance, a concentration of Arabic language newspapers, originally because of freedom from political interference, but helped considerably by easy access to a variety of distribution systems, together with access to copious and open supplies of information: libraries, news agencies, other media, other nationalities, etc.

Other forms of media have had a direct effect on the output

Nowadays there is radio and television being broadcast from London in most of the languages of the world. This is something that happened a long time before the world wide web (another British initiative) and which was arguably more important, if only because the proximity of information available in this way was always verifiable. (To quote my first editor, Malcolm Muggeridge, again: 'Don't give me the facts, give me the truth.')

It was this growing nucleus of information of all kinds within Britain that led William Haley, as the BBC director general, to have that essential conversation with a colleague after the second world war on ways of expanding the reach and influence of BBC radio and which led eventually to the creation of the BBC World Service, which now reaches 183m listeners every week. And it is this continuous conversation with the world over many years which has enriched, first, many branches of British media and, next, the vast majority of British citizens. As a result, for instance, wars to people in Britain no longer seem to take place in countries far away; they know just where they are, they may have even been there. This is certainly not true of citizens in America.

Another form of context that needs to be appreciated is that of competing media. As we have seen in the first part of this book, other forms of broadcast media have had a clear effect on BBC attitudes. But when the health of the directly competing media wanes it is obvious that BBC anxiety lessens. A major reason for an easing of competition is during a fall in advertising income. Because the BBC licence fee is stable, the Beeb can breath with ease. Of course, any effect on the Radio Four budget may well be the last to show as an outcome of this, but it is still a part of the enormous family, so is not immune to influence.

Little known specialist journals can make an important input

Right next door, so to speak, to Radio Four is Radio Three, from which it was so clearly separated in the 1960's. From time to time this also becomes a platform for speech radio, if potentially of a different kind, so clearly creates a context.

Another kind of context that counts is one I have already

referred to, the national press. Small (and declining) as its readership is, it usually seizes the advantage it undeniably has in being able to comment, as apposed to report, by trying to shape the national editorial agenda – what some call 'flying a kite'. For instance, it is hard to ignore the claim by a newspaper that it helped to win an election, even though everyone knows it as a lie. And certainly speakers are swiftly available to rebut such rumours by the national press, but they prefer to do this live on air, where their words will go out unchanged. So how can the BBC refuse? And how can Radio Four?

Of course, an important distinction between the BBC generally and other media is the lack of advertising. It goes without saying that the BBC's funding by licence fee provides a different and perhaps more reliable form of finance, but, much more importantly, in editorial terms this means that all BBC output can be more distant than its competitors from the pressure of commerce in planning programmes. There was once a time when print media was mainly driven by interest in public affairs. Now it is much more often a matter of providing a platform for product placement. Some newspapers are barely distinguishable from (extremely heavy) shopping catalogues. And, as print media are under increasing financial pressure, there is also a tendency to concentrate on low-cost lead stories casting doubt and suggesting scandals, rather than spending on original research. Radio Four need not follow these leads, but can find it hard to ignore them.

Also out there is the regional press, often with more readers than the national media, plus a growing number of specialist journals, largely - thank goodness - free of advertising and increasingly bought by subscription. These specialist journals are little known outside of their own specific audiences, but other journalists know them well, as they use them a lot for inside knowledge on all of their various subjects. Again, London is a major centre for international specialist media, all of which feeds into a central basket of concentrated resource. True, not all journalists use the basket, as they seem to find it hard to leave their computers and their easy access to on-line rumour, but those who care to make personal contact are inevitably rewarded.

What the BBC means to the rest of the world is often quite different to the British audience

An important personal experience was joining the staff of The Economist and being told by the editor that he never wanted to see me in the office, other than on press days, as he would then assume that I was not working: meaning collecting first hand information from specialist sources. Sadly, this is now rare in journalism. I hope for a revival.

There is also another political context, but this time with a small 'p'. Arguably London is also dominant in the provision of global organisations fiercely campaigning for free speech. To mention just five; Amnesty International, Article XIX, Index on Censorship, the media arm of George Soros' Open Society and the Institute for Peace and War Reporting. Their presence on the doorstep of the BBC is not accidental. Their values are shared and accepted. Alongside these are a multiplicity of specialist research bodies, such as the Royal Institute for International Affairs (at Chatham House), the Centre for European Reform, etc.

Oddly, there is also, already, an organisation called the BBC Trust (not to be confused with the successor group to the BBC governors) which has been in the business for some years of educating journalists and broadcasters in developing democracies, largely with the aid of European finance, on ways of doing business in the BBC style. The benefits of this to the BBC are too obvious to be explained.

Finally, there is the context created by the rest of the BBC, as the largest media organisation in the country, reaching into at least five kinds of media: television, radio, stand-alone programmes; on-line services; and publishing. This is particularly important when trying to define that allusive quality called reputation. Anyone who travels abroad will be told soon enough what people in other countries think about the BBC. But it will also, then, become clear that their vision of the BBC is seldom anything like yours.

Depending on their particular access to media, the BBC product they are mainly aware of could be: television programmes broadcast by and/or made with other companies; BBC English language lessons on tape; BBC books; BBC World Service broadcasts from London on long or medium wave or relayed around the world on VHF from over 1,000 transmitters; the BBC's six million pages of websites on twenty four platforms, with its biggest audience in the USA attracting five million hits a month (and visibly effecting mainstream US news coverage on Iraq, among other things); and the live or time-shifted download of particular programmes from another website. Only if they have spent time in the UK are they likely to have heard Radio Four broadcast directly on VHF or digital on the basis available to humble British licence payers.

Equally, radio listeners in the UK are unlikely to appreciate the BBC experience of people in other countries. It is true that listeners in the South East of England can pick up World Service Radio (financed completely by the Foreign Office) on medium wave, as it is beamed out across the continent. And more recently the World Service has been added to the Freeserve digital package available in the UK. But these are less the rule than exceptions.

Something that is certainly clear is that, when foreign visitors to the BBC drop in on Radio Four, with the idea of picking up some ideas for their own use, they are astounded by the complexity and expense of it all (at the last count, £10,500 an hour). They quickly realise that producing anything similar in their own countries, at least without the sale of advertising space, would be beyond their wildest dreams. They also discover, perhaps for the first time, that Britain is one of the few countries in the world where television is not the dominant media.

It can also be hard for a visitor to recognise the difference between BBC domestic radio and BBC world radio, partly because it so often sounds similar, partly because it is similar. Material from Radio Four and domestic radio news quite often finds its way onto the World Service, and vice versa. Which is another attraction of the Today programme for those speakers who may need to reach a worldwide audience.

Both networks follow the central BBC set of standards when it comes to balance and fairness and so on and it is common to hear the same voices, the same presenters, on both. It is mainly budgets that are different, with the annual £225 million provided for the World Service by the Foreign Office defining, not so much the content, but certainly the target audience.

If only because of the need to periodically negotiate the next World Service budget with the Foreign Office, the BBC has become very experienced, not just in negotiating with those in authority, but also in influencing the political climate for negotiation. Within this context, the image of the BBC is critically important. And so, also, Radio Four.

&

PRACTICE

Management

The continuous conversation known as Radio Four does not happen by accident. During twenty years as a freelance (outside) contributor to Radio Four programmes I also produced material for the Canadian Broadcasting Company, British Forces Broadcasting, the Central Office of Information, most of the other BBC and many other commercial radio stations, but I have to admit that I seldom paused to ask myself how programmes were planned.

There is a case for employing a consultant to employ consultants

Even when I became an independent programme maker I was doing little more than responding to what I saw as a defined need. Cause and effect seldom crossed my mind. And now I have to report, after some time spent more recently talking to commissioning editors at Radio Four, I am not too sure, in retrospect, that I was that much of an outsider. If Radio Four looks simple from the outside, I would suggest that it often looks much the same from the inside. People just do their work, don't they?

At the same time, an outsider could well be forgiven for believing that radio policy is created either by the chairman or the director general and that all programme content is planned by programme presenters. It is only after considering the total production costs (£67m pa) and the hours of programming (8,178 pa, with 6,366 hours coming from London, 1,540 hours from the rest of England, 43 hours from Northern Ireland, 163 hours from Scotland and 66 hours from Wales) that the need for a slightly more sophisticated system becomes more obvious. As with any other large organisation, delegation within the BBC is inevitable and happens in many different ways; although in this case dictated, it often seems, by reasons as haphazard as changes in the weather. And the first thing a new head of department does, of course, is to move all the chairs.

And moving chairs does have an effect. I think it was the management guru and religious broadcaster Charles Handy who told me the story of the effect of the clipboard: after time and motion experts watched the process of an assembly line they recommended a change in the light source, which swiftly produced an increase in output; the same exercise conducted a year later, recommending a return to the original light source, produced an identically swift increase; thus showing that the light had nothing to do with it, but that the men carrying clipboards - and paying attention to the workers - did. Such is the mystery of management. And consultants.

Inside the larger BBC it is darker. It goes without saying that the corporation is essentially a creative organisation. That much is obvious. What is a lot less obvious is that managing such a body is not like managing a conventionally commercial organisation. That should be obvious, too. The sad impression is that so often and for much of its life those in charge of managing the BBC have either not realised the difference or, more worryingly, have not been able to recognise the difference.

I speak from experience. Forty years ago, at the launch of Radio Four, British people, mainly accountants who believed they understood management (they had bought all the right books at airports, after all) were becoming just a bit edgy about the dramatic headway being made by a US management consultancy called McKinsey and Co. Not only had McKinsey been brought in to help re-plan the BBC, but they had also won contracts with The Bank of England, British Airways, Cunard and a whole raft of other British institutions.

On behalf of the worthy readers of the Sunday Telegraph, I was sent to interview McKinsey's tall, hawk-faced founding director in Britain, Hugh Parker. The secret of their success was quite simple, he said, and drew a number of triangles on a piece of paper for me, first one way up, then another way up. Like that, he said. I was none the wiser.

However, the strongest impression he left was of his appearance: he wore a bowler hat, a pin-striped suit and a rolled-up umbrella, quite unlike his British competitors, who generally wore American-style suits in bright, reflective hues. The way I read that was that he, as a consultant, was much more concerned with reassuring his customers than impressing them. Advice was something that came after winning the contract and, I suspect, depended mainly on what the client expected.

Years later, working at the National Economic Development Office on management education, I co-published some reports co-operatively with a completely new generation of McKinsey people: but, clearly, acceptability, although on a different plane, was still their primary objective.

This is not to suggest that anything done by McKinsey for the BBC has been in any way inept, simply that those who ordered the service may not always have been in possession of the full menu. Clearly, management can take the form of methodology or motivation, but it helps to chose.

Few in the creative industries have management training or ability

And yet, and yet, it is very interesting to note that McKinsey and Company decided to promote their considerable experience by publishing a Review of Public Service Broadcasting around the World, in 2004, which conspicuously failed, even once, to mention radio. One wonders what they learned.

In any case, the importance of being on the right wavelength for an audience is not a truth exclusive to management consultants so much as a general truth for all good managers. It is certainly common to all creative businesses. Witness the often furious turnover of editors at national newspapers. Gossip blown around after they leave is usually to do with a clash of opinion with their proprietors over current political issues. Not true. Few owners of newspapers care much about what goes into them. Their main concern is to publicly massage their egos by association with famous brand names, as well as, if possible, to make either a tax loss or a profit. But, as businessmen, they do know a bad manager when they see one. Which they do far too often.

The start of independent producers meant the start of commissioning editors

The sad fact is that the attitude appropriate for making a good journalist is usually quite unsuited to a good systems manager. A journalist is often a professional outsider, an irritant, a performer, with a tumbling supply of new ideas. None of this is terribly useful to reliable and methodical management.

On the other hand, the management of journalists, as with creative creatures of any kind, calls for a very particular talent. Temperament is a delicate flower that needs, on the one hand, to be kept within decent limits while, on the other, encouraged to bloom. The manager (controller, editor, producer, father figure) who can walk this particular type of tight rope is absolutely essential to the business of Radio Four. Especially because there are many programmes within this conversational outfit that are a long way from what would (seriously) be called journalism.

In the grey-suited days of Broadcasting House, at the birth of Radio Four, indeed, programme decision-making was casual and collegiate. Mutual trust between people was central.

Senior people had inevitably 'come down' from Oxbridge; secretaries all appeared to be the daughters of vicars; freelance contributors were reluctantly let in the door, but only if they could show without doubt that they came with the proper credentials. A chance meeting in the lift with a commissioning editor could then easily be a good time to suggest an input. He would certainly thank you, courteously, and ask for more detail, or else promise to reply very soon; a phone call would say yes or no.

I like to think that I had some sort of record for interviews used in Pick of the Week simply because I dropped tapes onto the desk of the Australian Margaret Howard, for many years the regular presenter, with the quiet suggestion that she might possibly like to use them. Every other week she did. I got no more money, but the exposure was invaluable in getting additional work. Now, in the jeans and tee-shirt era, when even director generals wear beards, the atmosphere has changed. In the past forty years Britain, and also the sentient part of the media which needs to be aware of Britain, such as Radio Four, has swiftly adjusted its clothing.

Within BBC radio in particular a major change has been the introduction of competition. To a certain extent there has always been some, between programmes and departments, as well as personalities, while a large proportion of presentation and production staff have always worked on a freelance basis, in one way or another.

Even director generals have been freelance – or worked on

contract, as they may prefer to say, dusting down their Armani suits. But the use of external programme providers has made a dramatic difference. The new compulsory allocation of a share of airtime to independents means that senior managers have had to learn to walk the walk and talk the talk of people who do not necessarily worship the more venerable of BBC conventions. The opposite is also true, of course.

One change caused by this was the appointment of commissioning editors just to handle external providers. These editors then have to compete with internal production editors in persuading controllers to take programmes. Fairly obviously, commissioning editors need different skills to production editors; you could say that they are more in the business of cautiously buying than generously spending; naturally, this effects their attitude.

Most importantly, the relationship of management to production staff is a sensitive issue that can have a very direct effect on the quality of output. On the one hand, within the BBC, it seems that purely administrative staff have often played a fairly passive role, which must have inevitably limited the value of their input. While the value of senior management would depend a great deal on their ability to handle both the (quiet) administrative and the (bullish) creative staff, as well as reflect the convictions and prejudices of their personal backgrounds.

The early BBC was run mainly by career civil servants; now it is run mainly by former journalists. This compares with the fashion for managers in newspapers, which swings on an almost annual basis between accountants, salesmen and journalists.

One could ask the simplistic question: why have managers?

Let me make a comparison. Some time ago I made an award-winning thirteen part radio series The right to work. It took over a year to make, included over a hundred interviews and was put together in my London apartment with a large pile of tapes, the occasional help of a production assistant and, finally, a recording engineer. Donald Brooks, who ran Radio Orwell in rural Ipswich, placed the programme with every independent station in the kingdom. When a producer for Radio Four's Analysis programme borrowed the tapes and broadcast an almost identical series a year later it then became necessary to (directly) involve editors, researchers, secretaries and other production staff, and (indirectly) schedulers, publicists, accountants, policy advisers, management consultants and controllers - at goodness knows what cost per hour. So which was the ideal process?

Intellectuals suddenly became more important than intellect

We all know that the British attitude to management is almost as uncomfortable as the British attitude to intellectuals, yet the reality remains that the large and complicated BBC would not work without them any more than would the National Health System. But size matters.

When Greg Dyke took over as director general of the BBC

(2000-2004) from John Birt (1992-2000) he found that administration was consuming 24 percent of income. He determined to cut this to 15 percent, but was pleased to see it fall to 12 percent, partly by severing all contact with management consultants, which saved £20m a year.

The didactic John Birt influence on BBC strategy had been a strange and remarkable experience and one guided by principles with which, by sheer accident, I seem to have had a close encounter. When the Canadian Lord Thomson owned The Times I was working on the business news desk. The newly appointed editor of that section was Peter Jay, the economist who later went on to be a presenter of Weekend World for the now defunct London Weekend Television.

'There is a need to run with the political tide' said one missive, mysteriously

I cannot remember Jay ever making an editorial decision on the business of the day, because his time seem to be totally dominated by much more interesting conversations with other staff members about such weighty issues as the meaning of monetary descriptors. We got every edition of the paper out every night all the same.

Equally, at Weekend World he developed a theory about British journalism in which he established that (all other) television contained 'a bias against understanding', which meant that reports lacked an explanation of context. His own broadcasts eventually made it clear what he meant by that, as most of his questions became longer than any possible answer.

Weekend World then developed a reputation – presumably among those who could not understand it – for intellectual excellence. Which, in my opinion, has a lot to do with how one of its producers, John Birt, graduated into being chief executive of the BBC, waving a large flag labelled 'a mission to explain.'

Birt joined the BBC as deputy director general in 1987, with direct responsibility for news and current affairs across the whole outfit, whereupon he instructed television and radio news to work in liaison. He also recruited a new layer of dual-media reporters with specialist knowledge. But the ground had already been laid for him by the previous director general Michael Checkland, who had set up internal BBC task forces largely in response to the growing political climate in favour of greater accountability in public bodies. And the BBC, of course, was a public body. One task force, called 'The BBC: The Entrepreneur' was justified thus: 'Beyond the needs of the consumer, there is a need to run with the political tide. Entrepreneurialism was a requirement of the 1980s and will still have an important part to play in the public sector in the 1990s.'

Accordingly, when John Birt became (an especially politically aware) director general he became even more enthused with management, apparently with the aim of making everyone and everything more accountable. Rules sprang up all over. Central to these were the Producers Guidelines, to be set alongside the Commercial Policy Guidelines, closely followed by Programme Strategy Reviews and then by Annual Performance Reviews, while inside every lavatory was (yes, you've guessed it) a Toilet Housekeeping Checklist. And no good management could survive, of course, without regular audits, so that audit managers had to be created for every level of activity.

Moving the chairs is one thing. What seemed to be happening on this occasion was the creation of a whole new warehouse.

Birt's successor, Greg Dyke, remembered his arrival at the BBC in his book Inside Story: 'What I eventually worked out was that this was an organisation that, at the top level, was risk averse. It commissioned more and more analysis and produced more and more papers to avoid taking risky decisions. The approach seemed, firstly, that the more analysis you understood the more likely you were to take the right decision, not something that I have ever seen proven. Much more importantly, and the reason why the reports were so lengthy, was that if the policy went wrong you could point to an exhaustive paper trail to protect you. It was classic civil service mentality.'

On the other hand, in the same book, Dyke admits to understanding the motivation: 'Publicly funded organisations are much more likely to avoid risk. The problem is that they are under much greater public scrutiny for the simple reason that they are spending public money. A single failure can be blown up by newspapers and politicians to such an extent that it does lasting damage to the organisation, or to its leader.

As a result, there is a real danger that public-sector organisations err on the side of caution and do not take the calculated risks they ought to take if they want to improve the services they deliver to the public. For the downside of a risk going wrong in a publicly funded organisations is public criticism, even public humiliation.'

All the same, Birt's succession by Dyke saw the chairs move again. Apart from sacking the consultants, he also attacked the system of departments charging each other for services, costing an average of £100 an invoice, by reducing internal cost centres from three hundred to sixty. External suppliers were reduced from 150,000 to 9,000. Accounting systems were cut from eleven to one. The finance department was cut from 1,000 to 500. While each department was ordered to produce its own plan for cutting overheads, which cut another 1,100 jobs and saved £166m. An eventual total saving of £480m a year then became available for investment in programmes, some of which, no doubt, found its way to Radio Four.

Don't mention the management, Dyke was advised

What this did to the efficiency of administration is a lot less clear. It is tempting to suggest that now there are not enough chairs to sit on. It is certainly hard to find a suitably quiet space in Broadcasting House to talk to producers. The smart euphemism for this is hot-desking. While producers who have to work in the new, open plan offices in the West London Media Village (consisting of the White City facilities centre, the programme producing Broadcast Centre and the management focused Media Centre) often have to take their mobile phones outside to make a coherent phone call. (Cold desking?)

The bizarre decision to move radio news, bulletins and programmes, to distant West London in 1998 at the declared cost of £41m was thankfully soon reversed, in the face of clearly demonstrated impracticality, which means it should all be back in Broadcasting House again by 2008.

The Birt regime also attempted to kill off all programme editors, in favour of a current affairs hierarchy which would allocate programme content (or 'product' as it was called) from a central control centre. Only a universal and noisy refusal by staff to play ball quashed the plan. Internal competition between programmes was clearly healthy, the creation of programme identities indispensable, the need to maintain speed in decision making crucial.

Radio Four is really a collection of fiefdoms, I was told by a helpful producer

When Greg Dyke made his opening address to staff on becoming director general he was advised by his personal publicity adviser not to mention the war of management, but to talk instead about programmes, the reason for their existence: the means of existence was thus overlooked and perhaps overlooked too far.

All the same, one definite improvement seemed to have happened, and that was encouraging staff to believe that they could manage themselves. Time was set aside for groups to brainstorm on ways of making work better. The simplest ideas were immediately adopted. In 2001 just 28 percent of people who worked for the BBC felt valued by it; two years later 58 percent did. Morale had begun to rise.

But what's essential to grasp about Radio Four, when it comes to understanding the management, is that the end result is one of compromise between a number of partners. As a senior producer explained to me: 'This is really a collection of fiefdoms'.

In between you can overlook the existence of a controller of BBC editorial policy who does not control policy, of a director of vision who does not direct vision, and a controller of knowledge who does not control knowledge. And so on. But such is the stuff of big companies.

Of course, there's also a controller of Radio Four who does in fact control Radio Four, Mark Damazer. But the news sequence programmes are the product of News (of which Damazer, luckily, was previously deputy director) which services all of the BBC. Other specialist programmes are also produced by sections working across all networks, for television as well as radio. While radio output as a whole comes under a director of audio and music.

When you think of it, this does actually make sense, in maximising expertise at the lowest possible cost. I once worked for a while for a government agency, the Central Office of Information, where one of my jobs was to handle requests for radio interviews with government ministers. One result was to have to make a decision on which of the 40-odd requests to allow for interviews on the same subject from 40-odd sections of the BBC. I soon pointed out the absurdity of this to former colleagues at the BBC (of my making this decision and not them) and not long after the idea was born to centralise news services. The downside of this, of course, is also clear, which is that the controller of Radio Four, among others, is never in complete control.

&

Programming

I had migrated as a freelance from BBC Radio London to Radio Four shortly ahead of the Radio London editorial director, who was going to head what was then called current affairs magazine programmes. Hence the producers on Radio Four were eager to know something about him, such as: was he any good at programming?

The question flummoxed me. I had no idea what programming was.

Later I understood why the question was important. Radio London, having at that time just one continuous strand of programmes and no direct competitor, was free to present any topic at any time, regardless of what anyone else did. The principle guidelines to bear in mind were the likely life and work patterns of the main, entirely locally interested audience, such as going to work between nine and five and probably not going to work at weekends.

On the other hand, Radio Four lives in a much more competitive environment, where there are not only work patterns to consider, but also the patterns of whatever media you think may be competing for your audience, as well as variations in interest by your audience in the very wide field of subject matter. (Would they like more science and less art, more humour and less drama, etcetera.) And above all that there is the continuous urge, on the one hand not to lose the existing audience, but to also gain a new one.

Clearly, audiences must change over time and when, as with Radio Four, most of them are in the older age brackets, a number are simply going to die, even if at a later date. Hence there are periodic drives to drive the average age of the listener downwards, not so much by targeting children so much as the twenty and thirty year olds. One way of doing this is by targeting the 6.30 pm space with what is meant to be a younger style of humour. The timing is important because it is an average time to return home - in fact, most might still be in cars - while it is too early to turn to television.

But media attempts to extend the age of audiences are often pushing against a brick wall. The fact remains that before people get married they usually have a more active than average social life outside of the home and, so, are often beyond the reach of fixed radio receivers. This may change with the increasing ability to hear radio on the move, but slowly.

Certain subjects also have a self-determining audience. Taking younger people again: because they travel more than most, and so make friends in other countries, they are generally more than averagely interested in international affairs. But once they form relationships and start buying homes and having children, their interest in foreign affairs inevitably gives way to domestic subjects such as health and education. Changing the style of reporting to attract a wider audience has seldom been successful. Above all that is the need to stay aware of the continuous evolution of society and the way in which it effects peoples' need to know and be entertained, which is largely reflected in the previous section of this book called 'From there to here'. Usually this is done through the simple process of regularly getting producers around a table and encouraging them to talk, which should at least capture their personal views. But at times there is a need to send somebody out to ask specific questions that produce measurable answers. Commissioning market research, its called.

The public seem to care less about the regional input so much as the regional output

Regionalism is part of programming as well, of course, although it used to be a more critical part than now. The early days of the BBC were in any case dominated by regional broadcasting radio stations that only occasionally joined hands, so to speak, to make a national station. This was partly because it represented the true state of the nation, with obviously different dialects and lifestyles in the various regions, which is no longer so true; but in any case this was before the launch of local radio, which has now effectively taken over the practical aspect of such things as local weather, travel and politics.

It is remarkable, however, that Radio Four still makes great efforts to delegate the production of programming to the regions. For instance, in 2005/6 London produced 6,339 hours of programming, the rest of England 1,553 hours, Scotland 133 hours, Wales 69 hours and Northern Ireland 41 hours. The public now seems a lot less concerned with the origin of programming so much as the content, but this does not deter the BBC from making a remarkable amount of noise about their regional activities, and the cost of it all, whenever locally elected politicians come near.

Some national programmes were made extremely difficult to produce because of regional opt-outs at various times of the day. Presenters of the Today programme were often confused by the need to allow for certain audiences to come and go at different times. Nowadays the nearest equivalent is pausing to remind the audience to change to a different wavelength for the longer version of the parliamentary report.

Programming also includes thinking of how to keep audiences that have already tuned in. Pre-announcing, or trailing, programmes is one way of doing this. Another is to place programmes in a sequence that ensures that each one compliments its companions, as well as allowing for competition in other media.

The advantage of producing parallel products, as the BBC does, is that each can be used to promote the others, if only by sharing and so reinforcing the brand name. More than that, they can also be used, usually free of charge, to carry specific messages about the others: advertising, publicity, whatever.

The BBC has had a lot of criticism about this in the past, specifically from publishers of journals in competition with

BBC titles; their complaints against the corporation using an unfair advantage were upheld, so that now unpaid cross-promotion of this kind has to be limited to BBC broadcasts. In practise what this produces is a regular amount of promotion for BBC television on BBC radio, but not, it seems, so much of radio programmes on television. I don't know whether this matters or not. I mean, not a great proportion of BBC1 viewers seem to be typical Radio Four listeners. But perhaps they aught to be?

Programming generally might well be thought comparable to conducting a symphony to be played in a motorway lay-by: every so often you need to have either a pause or a change of volume to allow for the passing traffic. Sometimes the passing cars have their windows open, sometimes not. Sometimes they will want to pause for relaxation, at other times press on. And so on.

In theory, the time-sensitivity of programming should become less important as other ways of accessing programmes, on-line and so on, become available. In practice, I suspect that the easier forms of access will always attract the biggest audience.

The printed media equivalent of programming is niche marketing. No print media editor in his right mind will try to aim his entire output to everyone in the country, or even to everyone over thirty, as Radio Four needs to. The choice of subject, the use of language, the selection of illustration should be aimed to attract a clearly identifiable group of people with an interest or attitude in common. And if there is competition for this slice of the market, then the stress should be on establishing a form of presentation which sets you apart from that competition. There is also the comparative luxury of providing some content which does not have to be consumed instantly, but which can be put aside and enjoyed later. Possibly much later. Radio is not like this.

However, radio does have the ability to use repeats, and Radio Four certainly seems to be much better at this nowadays. In particular, repeats generally follow within a day or two, but at a time of day opposed to the original broadcast. This means, for instance, that something that could have been heard by someone leaving their home to start a late working day could afterwards also be heard by someone returning home after an early working day.

All this is controlled by a number of people sitting at computers in what is call The Bridge, the control room for Radio Four which its at the prow of the ship-shaped Broadcast House, with the programme controller at the furthest outreach, in what they call The Mess, nautically of course.

&

Production

British broadcasters in general it seems attract a trust rating of 70 percent - which is not bad when compared with other journalists, who compete with politicians and estate agents as only 20 percent trusted professionals.

The main reason for this can only be the product: less likely to reach a conclusion without examining the evidence, more likely to offer a platform to a range of viewpoints. All because the whole process of discussion and debate lies at the heart of alive (in your living room, bathroom, bedroom, car) journalism. Static print journalism is forced to approach matters in a more didactic manner: first state the conclusion, then the (sort of) explanation.

Broadcast journalism need not arrive at a conclusion until the end of the programme, some time in the future. Also, print journalism that sells from counters on a casual basis (such as most newspapers in Britain) needs to attract its audience by headlining dramatic outcomes. Broadcast journalism attracts and holds its audience by welcoming and taking it into its confidence, holding its hand as it curiously walks around the scintillating garden of possibilities.

The BBC has an additional, particular role, of course, drawn from its tradition of impartiality, which has obviously also influenced its broadcasting competitors, who have not thought it wise to seem any less impartial. So a norm has been established.

All the same, the vast difference between print and broadcast journalism took me roughly two years to understand. Many years spent in middling and senior positions on prominent national newspapers and magazines were useful in opening the doors to Broadcasting House when the call was out for a supposedly better class of journalism in BBC radio, but not enough to prepare me for the stern realisation that nothing happens in broadcasting unless you can learn to persuade your subject, your interviewee, to say what they need to say. Print journalists can ignore the sad reality that most people in public life are effectively incoherent; broadcast journalists cannot. Production values are all.

Some of the best production ideas have come from studio engineers

Personally I avoided much of the problem by over-recording interviews and editing heavily, which certainly left me with a vast range of optional answers, but was of questionable value in terms of time management and even more questionable in terms of veracity. But at least no interviewee ever complained; they all seemed to think that what they had heard themselves say was in fact what they had said.

But all of this demonstrates the very special nature of radio. It is, if nothing else, a grass-roots process. The producer is king. Way underneath the director general, the network controllers, the various editors of various kinds, is the man or woman who handles the product, the live or recorded outcome on air: the radio producer. They research the story, they present to the editor, they negotiate with the subject, they commission the reporter, they report to the editor, they brief the presenter, they control the outcome, they take the flak for failure and (sometimes) the plaudits for success; all of this to a very tight time framework and while working unsociable hours.

For instance, on the Today programme, which is often described as the flagship programme for Radio Four, there is a staff of about fifty people to produce a three hour programme six days a week. On the production side this is made up of: the senior editor, who controls overall strategy and content; eight or nine commissioning editors, who work often in pairs on an occasional daily basis; plus about sixteen producers, who work a series of shifts, on days, evenings or nights, planning to produce or actually producing a number of items on a particular programme, working anything from a twelve to fourteen hour shift.

Inevitably for a daily programme of this length, the staff is about three times greater than for any comparable programme. Inevitably, for a programme with a voracious appetite, the decision-making process of what to run is strictly egalitarian, developed through the process of three editorial conferences a day. Contrary, it seems, to popular belief, the presenters on duty each day are often as surprised as anyone else on discovering who they are being asked to interview. There are national Sunday newspapers with smaller staffs. There are whole radio stations with smaller staffs. A potential competitor to the Today programme would need some generous pockets.

Studio managers are another essential part of the process. Some people call them engineers. In many cases they take up their jobs after good degrees in Oxbridge and often graduate to producers and editors. I have known some, indeed, move into television and the world of film. In my radio days many of the best production ideas have come not from producers but from studio engineers, who often turn out to have encyclopaedic knowledge of vast areas of culture, popular and otherwise, input from which can make all the difference between a fair programme and a good one.

Feeding into all this are endless lines of reporters and correspondents, some staff, many freelance, all of whom will be feeding their own lines of knowledge and interest into the production process at one level or another.

However, even senior editors are not at the top of the tree. They might be in commercial radio, but not in the much more prolific producer of words called Radio Four. Someone has to make sure that each programme knows its brief and does not overlap in speakers and ideas with other programmes. For Radio Four this means a controller, in charge of everything, plus a team of deputies and assistants to look after the practice and detail. Even then the controller has a various number of others over him, ranging from the head of radio to the director general.

But most controllers, just like editors of national newspapers, believe that their main job is to represent the interests of the listeners. How they physically do this is various. One way is to commission scientific research. The other is to invite the public to contact them.

In reality there are two reasons for broadcasters to invite their listeners to get in touch. One is to learn from their opinions. The other is to help create a communal atmosphere and so encourage the audience to believe that the programme belongs to them (which Radio Four listeners tend to believe anyway.) Sometimes the two go together, sometimes not.

The programmes belong to the listeners, of course, of course

It is not unknown in newspapers to create fictitious letters to the editor. I once had a comfortable living for a while on the Evening Standard ghosting letters from impoverished peers who were willing, for a consideration, to make nice noises about the publisher, Lord Beaverbrook. But I am sure this does not happen on Radio Four.

I suppose that all listeners to Radio Four would like their opinions to be noticed and taken seriously, whether sent by letter, message board or email. The trouble is that reacting to audience opinion is a complicated business. To do it properly calls for an understanding of motivation, in just the same way as interviewing people as part of a programme requires an understanding of their motivation. (For instance, you don't want to waste your time, or that of your audience, with talking to people who are insane. And you have to be very careful in talking to people who are professional trouble makers, who might possibly present more than their purely personal opinions, but who very probably do not.)

So how do you decide on motivation when all you have is a single declaration of belief from someone you have never met and know nothing about? Difficult. Possibly, if the point seems reasonable, the best course of action is to throw it into the public arena and see if it attracts support.

&

Presentation

When I told friends of my plan for this book, many of them suggested that, when I interviewed people for it, I aught to take a tape recorder. This assumes, of course, that any conversation on an interesting subject would inevitably produce material for an interesting recording. I thanked them and moved on.

Remembering that prompted this chapter.

It is strange, isn't it, that people with, say, a good camera think they can inevitably produce good pictures and that people with a decent tape recorder think they can produce a radio programme, but the same people, given some brushes and paint, do not think they can compete with a Rembrandt or a Rothko.

The fact remains, however, that an interview for print is greatly different from an interview for radio and the reason that programmes made for Radio Four are distinctive from those made for other networks is because the people who work on them have skills that others don't have.

A radio product has to be produced, of course. Which means arranging the conversation in such a way as to attract and keep the listener to the end. Obviously, in a real situation small talk about weather is an acceptable way of breaking the ice, but certainly not for a broadcast. Other than that, I think it took me about two years to be reasonably satisfied with the quality of my own work for radio, and that quality became no more than acceptable. The reason for this long learning process is because it takes time to learn to listen to yourself, as well as to others. And this is what makes good radio.

Also, while you are learning to listen, you must also learn how to coach those you are interviewing into saying what they need to say (in their opinion or yours) and in the right way. This calls for a combination of mental agility and appropriate verbal and body language.

In my opinion, radio is so much more revealing than any other medium precisely because it forces the audience to concentrate on the words, both in terms of logic and in terms of emotion, but without the pantomime of vision. I can play a recording back of my own voice and be reminded not only of what I said, but also of what I was thinking at the time. And when I play back a recording of somebody else talking I can make similar assumptions, however roughly, of what they were thinking at the time.

I have a strong feeling that everyone responds to radio in much the same way, however sub-consciously. And this is why the personality of a presenter makes such a great difference to the success of a radio programme. Controllers spend a lot of time worrying about this.

Take the distant formality of Jonathan Dimbleby, the camp clarity of Ned Sherrin, the quizzical air of Edie Mair, and the merry mischievousness of Laurie Taylor. It would be hard to separate their tones of voice from the subject matter of their programmes. But there are some programmes, of course, where the personality of the presenter is rightly not evident. Consumer programmes, for instance. Of course, one needs to feel that one can trust the bearer of good or bad tidings but, apart from that, the message is usually of greater importance than the messenger. It is principally with subjects where lateral thinking is important, such the arts, when it is useful to have a hint of the values held by the messenger. An interpretation is acceptable only when you can take the measure of the interpreter.

And whole books could and have been written about tones of voice and accents, using the voice as a musical instrument and so on. Nowadays, thank goodness, there is much less expectation that BBC broadcasts should be the reserve, or the graveyard, of placid Oxbridge English. Good communication nowadays is much more widely seen as the ability to connect with the listener on his terms, rather than try to impose a sense of values on him.

Whatever happened to Oxbridge English?

Clearly, then, the chemistry that makes a good radio programme is far greater than the totality of the words. And this, again, is where the skill of a good producer comes in. The job of a producer is partly to assemble the materials for a good programme, but also to develop a relationship with the participants which allows, indeed encourages, them to give of their best. And the principle tool for achieving this, especially while the programme is being recorded or broadcast, is through the skills of the presenter.

(In the best days of the Daily Express its editor Arthur Christianson insisted that the front page of every edition had to make people feel glad about getting up in the morning. Radio needs similar disciplines.)

And not all presenters are the same, of course. Which I suppose is a devious way of saying that not all presenters have the skills necessary for dealing with every situation. Some are too bullish, some too docile. Some interrupt too much, others not enough. Some can think for themselves, others get confused. And so on. Careful preparation and coaching is nearly always needed. Good presenters should feel in control. Good producers must be.

And, of course, there is always a continuous search for new presenters. Even stars cannot live for ever.

In commercial radio, where the total programme is usually run by one man on his own, this window on a long term view is seldom open. The station manager can listen in and express his views at the end of the programme, but then it is all too late, of course. The higher staff ratios at Radio Four are essential to the outcome.

&

PROGRAMME NOTES

Purpose

As this whole book is a personal portrait of an institution, so is this chapter a purely impressionistic snapshot of a number of programme genres. Clearly, with a book that will hopefully be kept as a record of its time, there is not much use detailing every current programme, if only because many of them will come and go. On the other hand, as talking about Radio Four without mentioning programmes is a little like talking about Marks and Spencer without mentioning knickers, what I aim to do is to select programmes that seem the most important to me, then group others which have a generic importance.

A word about cause and effect. There might be an impression that the controller of Radio Four is much like an editor of a rather large newspaper, which he is. But, also like a newspaper editor, he is physically quite incapable of personally supervising every input. There is far too much and it happens too quickly. Hence programmes are divided up into areas of common interest and management is delegated to section heads, who supervise the day to day process of production. How this actually happens depends a great deal, of course, on individual ability, so the chairs are normally in a state of continual change, together with job descriptions and titles. It is not unknown within the BBC to abolish complete departments, with their staff, because they do not work, and then reinvent and reappoint them under another name. This is easier than proving incompetence.

The controller also inherits a network, with some programmes boasting a lifespan of up to sixty years. As is well known, changing a simple theme tune is quite enough to inspire an absolute avalanche of fiery reaction, so that changing a programme might (who knows?) lead to a complete and utter breakdown in communication between the public who, after all, own the programmes and the producers who simply provide them. Hence, evolution is the principle option open to a keen controller, rather than what might be seen as a revolution. So Radio Four rolls on.

All the same, it might be useful to add some perspective with a list of generic programme types in order of their contribution of programme hours per year as of the last count. Using BBC categories rather than mine: News and weather 2,374. Factual 1,391. Current affairs 1,147. Drama 1,076. Sport 793. Entertainment 494. Arts 474. Religion 271. Schools 169. Children 26. Presentation 21.

Today

For many people the Today programme is Radio Four. Or at least the most prominent part of it. Even if it was born ten years before Radio Four. Sorry to bang on about London again, but at the latest count Today's early morning share of radio listeners in the capital was 20.3 percent, compared with 13.8 percent for Terry Wogan on Radio Two and 5.6 percent for the Capital Radio breakfast show. To get that kind of audience, the editor of any national newspaper would seriously think of sacrificing his right arm. As it is, the best they can do is to forward early copies of their newspaper to the programme, in the hope that, through quotation, at least some of it can reach that bigger public. The editor of the Daily Mail, arguably the most influential newspaper of middle England, openly admits his admiration. ('I, for one, would pay the licence fee just for Radio 4'.) Which just may be because he knows that his target audience (that is, people in the higher income brackets) are normally twice as likely to get their news from radio than from television or newspapers; and especially from Today.

Meanwhile, the press officers of innumerable public and private enterprises have programmed their recording machines to copy every minute of the three hour long programme, ready to spring into reactive mode the moment their masters demand it. At the same time, senior civil servants are listening hard for public image justifications for their most awkward proposals, editors of competing media are poised to exploit even the most tenuous of agenda items that could be classified as news, opinion formers in all walks of life have their hands outstretched for anything to reassure themselves and anyone else that they really do have the ability to form opinions, while thousands of people on their way to work, at home or away, are slowly adjusting themselves to the reality of yet another day which may, just may, have a framework already formed that would make that day just a little bit different from the day before. They are seldom disappointed.

Anyone desperate to experience by proxy the mechanics of putting the programme together could do worse than read All our Todays by Paul Donavan and Woman of Today by Sue MacGregor. My own experience reaches back to the days when the managers first introduced a Saturday edition, but none too seriously. The self-consciously dashing Michael Aspel, heavy with jewellery over his partially closed black silk shirt, would lightly tease the female production staff while discarding any input that he thought too heavy for a pleasant weekend.

There was also originally only one presenter during the week, notably the notoriously incompetent but charming ex news reader Jack de Manio, who sometimes took wine with me at The Queens Elms in the Fulham Road, together with the novelist Laurie Lee, who was at one time anxious to accept an advance from his publisher to retrace his experience of Spain, but lacked the ability. 'I have forgotten my Spanish and I can't drive' he said. He was looking, of course, for a pretty girl who could do both. Jack invited him to ask for help on the programme. After the broadcast, my next meeting with Laurie at the Elms revealed that he was far too frightened to open any of the six sacks of mail he had received ('how can I turn down so many women?), so I invited him to take my 18-year-old girlfriend at the time, which he did. The programme was altogether more casual then. Today was launched on 28 October 1957 from an idea mooted by a former barrister and BBC trainee called Robin Day, who weeks later moved to television; he simply pointed out the obvious truth that there were bound to be more people accessible to what was then called a wireless set in the morning than at any other time.

And so it began, in the form of two twenty minute sections, at 7.15 am and 8.15 am, in what was still the Home Service. But the more heavyweight news programme for many years was The World at One, steered from its start in 1965 by the heavy breathing William Hardcastle, who had been plucked, if not exactly fresh, from the editor's chair of the Daily Mail. His slurred vowels shocked conventional broadcasters, but his impolite need to know impressed listeners.

The first controller of Radio Four, Gerry Mansell, had been determined to boost the intellectual content of news coverage, to drag it out of the tradition of subservience, and the then common habit of inviting Fleet Street figures to help put the news into context made it obvious that some of them would be rather better on the other side of the microphone. After all, it is difficult to get the right answer when the question is wrong. Other Fleet Street hacks such as Alistair Osborne and Julian Holland became equally important as programme editors. It took some years for the Today programme to develop a similar weight.

The controller of Radio Four after Mansell, the ex-intelligence officer Tony Whitby, was even more eager to beef up the intellectual content. Given that Whitby had a parallel life as a playwright, it seems odd now to recall that, after his five years in office and sudden death from cancer, his successor, Ian MacIntyre, immediately determined that that there was far too much serious talk on the network, so proceeded to cut the (by then, longer) Today programme in half. He is still remembered as Mac the Knife. Filling the yawning gap in between must have been one of the hardest jobs in radio. It was given to the optimistically named continuity department, run by Jim Black. It did not take long for BBC management to move the possibly over-erudite Ian MacIntyre to the rather more speech light Radio Three, so that Today could be put back onto its continuous track.

However, once de Manio had been sacked, for drinking, wrong time-keeping or whatever, in 1971, the programme developed muscles. The approach of breakfast television provided a useful spur, as well as a bigger budget. A virtual galaxy of presenters was then imported (Robert Robertson, Brian Redhead, John Timpson, Peter Hobday, Sue McGregor), the pattern was adopted of joint presentation, then normal in the USA, and it became (publicly) known that regular listeners included such people as the Prime Minster and The Queen.

Perhaps more delightfully, when the elegant Virginia Bottomley was health secretary for the Conservative government and appeared on Desert Island Discs she declared that her one luxury, were she to be deserted, would be a constant supply of the Today programme. Bless her.

It would be invidious to suggest that either a presenter or an editor provided the most important input to the programme over any period of time, but there is little doubt that Today first became a serious force in the land during the presentational tenure of the former Guardian northern editor Brian Redhead, who started in 1975.

As his obituary in The Times later said: 'Redhead made Today a programme that no member of the political class could miss. The beneficiary . . . was the very medium of radio'. As his colleague Sue MacGregor said: 'He knew that one of the secrets of sounding good was being able to put on a bit of a performance, and his enjoyment of that theatricality was infectious. He was also maddeningly cocksure, bumptious and a show-off and could be infuriating to work with. On occasion he was quite frighteningly pugnacious, and there were times when he almost came to blows with his overnight editor. At the very least he called everyone with whom he had the slightest disagreement a "prat".' He also had a habit of receiving detailed background briefings by immediately throwing them away.

There is some evidence to suggest that John Humphrys, who worked alongside Redhead for a while, learned a great deal from him. Humphrys had been recruited from television and had only a modest amount of radio experience at that time. Nowadays 'Hurumphrys' when confronted by a politician is described as a master of 'magisterial distrust'.

Of course there are love/hate reactions to particular

presenters, but that's the ideal kind of reaction to have, surely? A presenter with a tone or attitude that is not challenging would be of little use in front of interviewees who refuse to be challenged. A kind of boldness had in any case been developed in the 70s and 80s that, on the one hand, rather frightened potential studio guests, but also flattered them by making their subject areas that much more interesting. A considerable subsidiary industry soon began in outside studios with Today presenters training potential interviewees in the art of interviews, although this was ended, quite properly, in 1995.

The 90's became a period when external interest in the programme reached a peak in terms of attempts to influence its content. Pressure from political parties was particularly strong, with frequent telephone calls designed to persuade producers to field one presenter rather than another. Complaints to all levels of management about the treatment of interviewees also increased in frequency. Peter Mandelson for the Labour party always seemed to know what was planned ahead of broadcast and once spent a whole hour on the phone in an effort to influence the format. He failed.

Alastair Campbell, as the Prime Minister's spokesman, regularly insulted the programme at his press briefings, describing it as the product of a 'downmarket, over-staffed, over-bureaucratic, ridiculous organisation', although this did not stop him trying to use it. More substantially, members of any party in government can always imply, if not actually say, that the BBC's right to continue to exist is always at stake.

External observers would call this bullying. Programme staff are inevitably flattered at this perception of their power.

A more sympathetic source of complaint is from someone asked to take part in the programme, who sets apart time and prepares for the meeting, possibly travelling a great distance, only, at the last minute, to be rejected. This can happen to even the most important people. Unfortunately, it is inevitable within such a long, complex and changing production. Items over-run and priorities change as the news agenda develops. Staff reporters can be called from their beds to the telephone several times over several hours, each time poised to voice a report and each time to be turned down.

The programme for much of its life ran for two and half hours. Since 1988, in an effort to hold on to this valuable audience, it has run to three, even though few listeners are expected to stay with it all of the way through. This is why it is planned to have a balance of tone within each half hour sequence, with a certain amount of repetition from one sequence to another of the harder type of news. Within the Today office, the prize spot is always seen as 8.10 am, after the essential weather and news bulletins, which is when the main live interview is scheduled, planned to last for rather more, sometimes a lot more, than the standard three minutes. Some 300,000 listeners overseas are said to download this daily as a podcast. There is a sort of silent competition between presenters for this spot, but the editors of the day have to make a decision based on their own view of best fitting the subject to the questioner. Other key moments are at 7.10 am and 7.30 am, also after the weather and news.

The senior programme editor may not even be in at that time, although he can monitor the production progress on-line. But he will be in the studio before the end of the programme, which is when he may suddenly meet for the first time a scattering of famous public figures, still waiting for their turn in front of a microphone.

The tension in the studio and production office while the programme is on air is intense, not unlike the atmosphere offstage during a ballet performance, with prima donnas flitting on and off and support staff anxiously hovering. In these circumstances, any humour is remarkable.

Nevertheless, humour there definitely is, alongside the continuous juggling act of slotting recorded interviews in-between live interviews, business, sport, religion, the papers, whatever.

Afterwards there will be an editorial meeting to analyse the day's work and to lay out a schedule for the 20-odd items needed for the following morning, based on the diary of pre-announced events. Long distance planning and the listing of key contacts are specific production functions. There will be another editorial meeting in the afternoon, when producers will report back on progress in making the items real. After this, the schedule will be handed over to the night editor, whose job it is to make sure that everything possible is lined up in shape and in time for delivery, in the course of which he will stage his own editorial meeting. Everyone works in shifts, of course.

Meanwhile the presenters have gone off home, or wherever it is they choose to go, and usually aim for an early night, to help them get up in the morning. So as not to miss a normal evening social life, Brian Redhead used to go completely to bed for two hours every afternoon. Presenters need to be in the studio by four in the morning, ready to read themselves up on their subjects and to write their introductions for the start of the programme at six. Some have breakfast. Most do not but nibble through the programme until it ends at nine. Cold slices of toast and packets of jam are not unknown additions to the office furniture.

The lead-in to an item on Today has to be very carefully constructed by the presenter, in order to go as quickly as possible to the heart of the subject, with the aim of moving the story on, so setting the national news agenda. A more recent editor, Kevin Marsh, described it as the target of always asking the unasked question.

The ability of the programme to affect the national news agenda is demonstrated in at least two ways. One is that the content of the programme is usually debated in Whitehall even before it has ended, at a meeting of government heads of information for various departments who have the Today running order in front of them; they need to weigh the influence that the outcome of the various interviews will have on public and political opinion. Another effect might also be born at the same meeting. Its main purpose is to co-ordinate their various announcements for the following day, but they will also have to decide to what degree to try to use the programme in this process.

Once upon a time major announcements were offered to the world at ministry-based press conferences, with a lot of effort spent in the weeks before until agreeing on a single statement called a press release. Every editor would send a reporter to the event, who would humbly accept the release and scarper back off to their offices to prepare their stories. Nowadays press conferences are poorly attended because they are generally seen as counter-productive, if only because of the time and physical effort needed to attend them. And being given the same story as everyone else is definitely seen as an implied insult to a self-consciously competitive journalist.

Nowadays the preferred route for media advisers is to plant in the programme an advance notice (leak?) of the fuller statement to come, usually through a friendly reporter, partly in order to generate a wider appetite for the story, partly in the hope of steering the subsequent news agenda in a favourable direction. The subsequent follow-up from journalists can then be handled discretely, with the aim of spreading the result as widely and variously as possible. For many stories there is no better place to do this than on the Today programme; its audience profile is ideal.

Editors of Today have their own objectives, of course. One of which is to use their privileged position to not only be first to alert the nation to an imminent event, but to also steal a lead on other media in identifying the most important aspect of the story, whatever its authors may prefer to say.

The preparation for this is inevitably delicate. Clearly there has to be some agreement on the area to be covered, in order to produce an interviewee, and there will probably be some agreement on the type of questions to be asked and the order in which they will come. Not to do this could produce an awkward silence, which would be a waste of time for everyone. Both sides will then quietly polish their ideal words and phrases, conscious all the while of the limited amount of time available.

Lack of time is, of course, the main reason why some interviews have to be abruptly ended, which always leads to complaints. But even the most careful joint agreements before going on-air can go awry when speakers are suddenly inspired to have more thoughts with, of course, many more words.

In recent years audience research has shown that listeners particularly care about the maintenance of manners, so easily forgotten by the London-based team, so that a 'Good morning' needs to precede every interviewee and an apology needs to follow every interruption, however much it may have been necessary. But what neither partner to a Today discussion will reveal to the other is their secret weapon, which they will each hope to release at just the right time to produce the right (emphatic) effect. This will appear impromptu but never will be. This is what the listeners like.

The sad fact is that the liveliest interviews of this kind inevitably involve politicians, partly because, through practice, they can usually be relied on to give good verbal value (Edward Stourton: 'To put it cynically . . .' Sir Michael Heseltine: 'Well, if you weren't cynical you wouldn't be in the Today programme. I accept that at once.'), partly because they are always available. Dozens of them. This means that the people who actually run the country (such as civil servants, businessmen and farmers) as opposed to those talking about it, hardly ever get a look in. (The business slot, of course, is seldom about business, so much as gambling on business.) My own belief is that this adds to a generally exaggerated expectation by the public of the importance of politicians and, hence, to an equivalent disappointment when it becomes evident they simply do not have the ability to deliver on their ideals. Today has a lot to answer for.

Equally, people working for other programmes can weary of having to explain to potential interviewees that their programme is not like Today and that, if they were come into the studio, John Humphrys will not jump out of the microphone and bite them. That is something to answer for, too.

All the same, it is worth while repeating the inspired assertion in Paul Donavan's All our Todays that the programme is 'a distinctive dawn caucus'.

The Archers

It is a well-known if uncomfortable fact that you cannot please all of the people all of the time, and The Archers is a programme which proves that exactly. It may well be that this is one of Radio Four's most popular programmes, but why is it that I don't know anyone who listens to it? Indeed, when I ask around it produces the same expression on many people's faces as it probably produces on mine. Shall we call it a wince? When I ask why, they normally mumble something about the theme music, but I don't believe that. I happen to feel that this is a perfect preparation for the programme: replete with simple goodwill and absolute predictability. Brookfield Farm in Ambridge, situated in the fictional middle of England between Borchester and Felversham is just as secure, wise and warm as anyone could wish. And very, very ordinary. I suppose it is what the once angry and young playwright John Osborne would have called Loamshire.

Mind you, I am not against soap operas. Perhaps my problem is that I was brought up on the forerunner of The Archers: Dick Barton, Special Agent. Admittedly this was specifically for children, but at least it contained what I consider to be the essential ingredients for any soap opera (which, after all, were invented in the US for the purposes of selling soap): fast and unpredictable action, ending with an absolutely essential life-threatening cliff-hanger. The world could not go on unless you tuned into the next episode. On the other hand, you can miss whole weeks of The Archers and nothing ever seems to have changed. Knowing that thousands of listeners like it this way only depresses me more. In my mind it just does not fit into the lively and enquiring format for the rest of Radio Four.

After Dick Barton there were a number of other serials with varying life spans. Mrs Dale's Diary was one, set in the home of a suburban doctor, which I suppose set the scene for invariable ordinariness, if it were not for the potentially offensive middle-class attitude of his wife, Mrs Dale. So many listeners felt excluded by this. (The Czech-born Tom Stoppard, who began his bizarre but lucrative playwriting career on the BBC, was judged insufficiently sympathetic for Mrs Dale's Diary, so moved to working for the BBC African Service, writing a series about foreign students in Britain. And who is laughing now?)

The brief for The Archers was originally one of pure propaganda, to induce post war households to think more creatively about their limited food supplies. It is still not averse to supporting national causes germane to agriculture, but only if they seem appropriately topical. At least it does reflect the major themes of the day. It is just that the mirror is not as clear as it might be.

And the amount of work that goes into what seems a simplistic programme is very impressive. The precedent was set very early here by the BBC's north of England controller Jock Gallagher when he created a document that charted the exact detail of this virtually real community in precise detail (names, addresses, proximity, relationships) to ensure that scriptwriters over the years could maintain absolute consistency.

The harshest comments I have heard about The Archers have come from farmers, not on terms of agricultural so much as social unreality. But, then, I suppose that specialists of any kind are not their own best interpreters.

All the same, there is no denying that, after the news and the Today programme, The Archers attracts a stronger following than any other programme on Radio Four, even including the royal family (the programme's theme tune should become the national anthem, say some overseas listeners). And it boosts the network audience. I guess it primarily attracts the kind of people who like to lead their lives through others, people who read novels. It is also by far the most popular of all radio programmes to listen to on-line, with over a million monthly downloads. But whether it would be more comfortable on Radio Two is a debate that has yet to happen.

Consumer

Dull, dull, dull say the glitterati of Broadcasting House of consumer programmes. Yes, yes, of course. Just as are bankers, doctors, teachers and, let's face it, cooks. But how would we live without them? And is dullness not really in the eye of the beholder?

The context counts. Within the BBC as a whole there is an undeniable intellectual snobbery about meeting Famous People. Which means, by implication, that news programmes are of course more important than consumer programmes. This no doubt stems from the time when journalists first start their careers and go home to tell their mothers, wives, girlfriends, about having met this or that well-known person. It seems to make all that tedious effort of training and qualifying worthwhile, because the people around you can now especially admire you. Meeting important people makes you important, doesn't it? Well, young people think like that. But it's a bit sad when journalists well advanced in their careers fail to reach maturity.

But a look at the number of regular or semi-regular programmes on Radio Four with a consumer bias surely indicates more than a little general interest in the basic business of life. The fact that they rarely feature brilliant arguments with professional debaters is not a detraction, but a benefit. Indeed, rumour has it that the audience appreciation figures, which are tasted every month by the BBC but not released externally, show a higher value by listeners put on programmes such as You and Yours than even Today or Woman's Hour.

It is reported that the first radio consumer programme, called Can I help you? was produced in 1939 by Guy Burgess, who was later to become rather more famous as someone who wanted to help the USSR. In partnership with this innovation were the newly formed Citizens Advice Bureau, the Trades Union Congress and the National Council for Social Service. Listeners were invited to write directly for advice to the CAB, but many of them wrote directly to the BBC, and the NCSS contributed £10 to each programme to meet the cost of this. In 1970 the programme was re-named You and Yours, which is still its name today.

Eventually sixteen different radio and television programmes were on air with some facility of taking enquiries from the public, with the result that in 1995 the BBC decided to centralise the facility, if only to be sure that calls could be answered for most of the working day. Nowadays the BBC Helpline takes calls from eight in the morning until twelve at night, pointing people to specialists in a whole range of subjects. This was originally run by an educational charity called Broadcasting Support Services, which in 2001 outsourced the entire operation on a ten year contract, at a cost to the BSS of between £2 to £6 a time. However, as people have become increasingly confident with the world wide web, the need to provide information in this way has begun to fall, with the latest annual total of calls at about 200,000.

Meanwhile, consumer programmes have shown themselves just as capable of influencing such things as government policy as any other medium. I can think of a campaign on You and Yours which revealed the dirty tricks of the sugar lobby to besmirch artificial sweeteners: that left a lot of naive politicians with egg on their faces. I can remember an interview with a government environment minister which showed that his claims about clean water on British beaches were totally bogus. I can also remember the joy of broadcasting his anger. He was demoted the following week. And I can remember embarrassing British banks when they tried to force their more passive customers to accept credit cards, leading to helpful legislation soon after which banned the practice. And so on.

The reality is that both British companies and British government departments are having to be much more careful in their relations with their customers as a direct result of consumer journalism, in which Radio Four has been a conspicuous leader. I mean, it is not that long ago when banks actually made it hard to open an account; intimidation was the norm.

Soon after You and Yours began it gave birth to a number of less frequent but harder hitting investigative programmes, within which obvious villains were held to account. Many minutes of heavy breathing soon began to invade the airwaves, recording the valiant efforts of reporters to catch up with absconding villains before they could hide behind their heavy doors. And it was not long after that before television producers realised what sensational programme material they had been missing, so carried on the theme.

But consumer programmes, by my definition, are not confined to shopping. I also include education, medicine, personal finance, travel, industrial relations, even the application of science. The wealth of applicable information which is provided on a regular basis on Radio Four is impressive. The fact that most of this is not delivered via government spokesmen or with a political spin is an advantage, not a limitation.

And then, of course, you have the old soldiers in the army of convinced producers of programmes for the common good, such as the ageless financial journalist Vincent Duggleby, who at one time combined working for the (now defunct) Financial World Tonight with a whole battery of personal finance programmes, managing to make all them sound remarkably coherent and logical. His reputation for financial sagacity was not confined to his professional life, as was shown by his adherence to travelling by bicycle and reportedly filling his home garage with the latest scarce commodity, such as coffee or sugar. Not many journalists are that sincere, alas.

The God slot

Please pardon the slang, but The God Slot as an unofficial title seems to have been used at the BBC for as long as I can remember and I happen to find it charmingly irreverent. The precise label refers only to the brief talk slotted into the Today programme, but it has to be considered, of course, in the much wider context of religious and ethical broadcasts across the board and throughout the week. Incidentally, at one time the god slot was a more popular part of the Today programme than either sport or business, probably because, when well done, it engages the little grey cells rather more than the recitation of statistics.

All the same, the subject area is one that attracts rather more heated discussion than most topics, despite the distinctly accommodating tone of much of the output. I suspect that this is largely for traditional reasons, insofar as a major proportion of the Radio Four audience spent their early years in the restrictively religious climate well known to the first director general, John Reith, and which has for ever since been resented for having been responsible for so many years of gloomy Sundays. That aside, it also depends on the stand that a person takes on the proper place of religion in society.

However, it is many years since Reith insisted on regular space being found for the promotion of the Christian gospel. For at least the past fifteen years the regular output has included time for all religions and none, if that is how you would describe atheism. Many non-Christian groups are now into their third generation as immigrants, so need a different focus to their parents. The output also includes space for subjects that are not connected with faith and spirituality so much as belief, meaning ethics. Think of Something Understood, The Moral Maze and Beyond Belief.

I personally find Something Understood as one of the most truly cultural programmes on the network, combining as it does well-delivered prose, poetry and music, as well as the carefully developed links between each item that often challenge basic beliefs. The Religion and Ethics department and its staff of thirty produces programme material for all of the radio stations, but most is for Radio Four. Most of that is for regular programmes, but there are also a fair number of one-offs, looking at life-styles and so on, some of which are among the top five most popular programmes.

So much is produced, in fact, that it is really misleading to label the subject as a slot. The regular programmes alone demand 534 hours of material a year.

Some of this, of course, is simply broadcasting services from churches, which might sound easier than it is, because, however much some people may groan at the idea of listening to a typical church service, the programmes that go out are the result of years of annotated experience of encouraging the clergy to improve their public speaking. And it must have worked, as Sunday Worship, for instance, now has an audience, at 1.7 m, double that of Newsnight on BBC1 television.

The God slot on the Today programme was originally recorded, but one day the wrong tape was played, a Christmas talk at Easter or something, so has been delivered live ever since, despite the many and various problems of getting different people into different studios at different times all over the country. And of course there is always the difficult problem of 'resting' certain eminent speakers when they are thought to have done their best; but that's what producers are for, of course. Personally I hope that Rabbi Lionel Blue will live for ever. I remember suggesting to the London Business School that the only way they were likely to get their difficult existence mentioned on the Today programme, assuming that they had an academic with religious leanings, was to offer his services as speaker for the God slot. Professor Charles Handy shortly after launched his long and successful career as a broadcaster. I believe the LBS is still in business. Somebody must be watching over them.

Any questions

I have this problem. I am confused between Question Time on BBC television and Any Questions on BBC radio. I know that one is presented by David Dimbleby and the other by Jonathan Dimbleby. I know they are both the sons of Richard Dimbleby, who was virtually the voice of the BBC in the Grand old Days. Wars, coronations, funerals and all that.

And I remember sitting next to their mother at a book launch at the Dorchester hotel (the book was an autobiography by Wilfred Pickles, who admitted to me that he had never met his next door neighbours) and her seeking my advice, as an obviously experienced journalist, on how on earth she was going to get her son away from wearing cardigans and living on vegetables in a tent in a field and into a proper job, such as running the family newspaper business.

But I have no memory of which son she was talking about. What I do remember, however, is her indomitable insistence on demanding that I, as a complete stranger, give her an answer on what, to me, seemed a purely personal matter. So much like her sons, I thought. And her husband, too, probably.

If there is a middle class characteristic in Britain today, then perhaps this is it. Nobody has the right to be modest or discreet or admit ignorance. On the contrary, it is the right of others to know what is in your mind. There must be something there. Open your mouth. East your greens. Sit up and answer clearly. I insist. It is what you might call an imposed democracy.

I have this dream that suddenly all the media study schools in the country (and there are a lot) stop examining the entrails of the Hutton Report and instead start studying Question Time. But now they use as a reference, not just one newspaper report, but all of the many and sophisticated technical means available to them to trace the cause and effect of every news story mentioned on Question Time over the previous seven days. The aim is obvious. It is simply to decide, without doubt, whether the chicken came before the egg.

Put it this way. The questions asked by members of the audience at Question Time, obviously carefully selected by the producer, are always based on the major issues of the day. While the answers from the panellists, also obviously carefully selected by the producer, are always based, or so it seems, on the awareness level already associated with those speakers. The point is, or seems to be, that both the audience and the panellists need to be equally dependent on popular perception, meaning the media, on what has happened in the first place. And neither side are expected to be experts. Put another way, both sides are expected to be equally ignorant.

Of course, that does not deter the panellists (if only because they are guarded by a table) from assuming an air of greater wisdom.

And this is where the Dimbleby skill kicks in. As the media students will no doubt discover, the story, whatever it is, first saw the light of day in, say, a newspaper. It was then repeated in other newspapers and other media. As this usually involves asking for a reaction from interested parties, one of those reactions may very well become more interesting than the original story. The reaction then becomes the story. And so on.

Hence, by the time the stentorian tones of a Dimbleby demand an explanation, or at least an evaluation, the story itself has become like a piece of putty, which provides ample scope for everyone on the programme to move into completely different issues, all based on supposition, mainly based on fiction. Tempers are tested, swords are crossed, voices are raised, emotions are stirred.

Great stuff for the self-important.

A media studies student could file thousands of words on possible cause and actual effect. But only the likes of a Dimbleby can firmly insist on clarity.

But wait a minute. My memory is playing tricks again. Now I hear the extremely strict diction of Freddy Grisewood as chairman of the programme. And now his successor, the melodious former disc jockey David Jacobs. Was the programme really any better? I honestly can't remember.

Parliament

There are politics and there is Parliament. As far as the BBC is concerned, for operational reasons the two areas are separate. Politics is the daily kerfuffle of assertion and counter assertion that is treated as part of the general news agenda. Parliament is the formal obligation accepted by the Corporation to provide a regular record of business as conducted by elected politicians within the Houses of Parliament, as well as (nowadays) in Wales, Scotland and Strasbourg. The first depends on the judgement **of general news editors on the amount of time to be spent on each item, while obviously** taking guidance from their political specialists. The second depends on a completely different set of handlers, who see themselves as producing something more like an audio version of the official report of parliament, Hansard. An excellent account of how this came about can be found in the book Order! Order! Fifty years of Today in Parliament by Mark D'Arcy.

The early morning report Yesterday in Parliament has been something of a political football in recent years. It has gradually been squeezed out of the Today programme, or at least reduced to the slimmest of summaries, with a referral to a fuller and more impressionistic version on long wave. Some call this the irritating version. But personally I cannot anyway remember ever owning a receiver with the ability to get long wave. All the same, the more factual and useful Today in Parliament, going out in the evening on VHF and digital, manages to attract an average daily audience of about 500,000, which does not suggest an audience only of egotistical MPs.

The unit in charge of this basic reporting, like many others in the BBC, deploys its staff across all media: Freeview, satellite, cable, online and the various forms of radio, which produces an almost unbroken flow of information for every day of the week. After all, the British parliament sits for longer than most parliaments in the world, so there is rarely a shortage of input. The correspondents are not expected to add perspective, but to simply select the current business that seems the most important.

The style was established in 1944 by William Haley as director general, who seemed keen to head off the emerging ambition of Parliament to establish rules for BBC reporting which may have been too strict for comfort, so he pre-empted them by primly ordering that the then current journalistic fashion for ironic Parliamentary sketches be side-stepped in favour of simplicity and sobriety. (What this means in effect is that when the voices of politicians speaking in the Chamber are used as part of a summary they may not be edited in the official report, meaning Today in Parliament, however incoherent they may naturally be as speakers.) Nevertheless, Parliament took the precaution of guarding against any possible change of heart within the BBC by writing the need for regular parliamentary reporting permanently into the Charter: with the daily parliamentary report being the only programme thought important enough by politicians to be specifically mentioned.

It is interesting to remember that before the Second World War there was no broadcast reporting of Parliament. This relatively new technology was considered dangerously frivolous by most politicians. Only during the War, in the 1940s, was it thought possibly desirable to allocate two seats in the press gallery to the BBC, but only on condition that they asked permission to attend each morning from the Sergeant at Arms and also if they promised not to take notes. As the seats were anyway too far away from the floor to see or hear anything very much, their usefulness was more symbolic than actual.

The BBC had to rely mainly on the Reuters news agency for detailed reports, until allowed access to the war damaged but rebuilt House of Commons, when they were pleased to find that they had been given two seats at the very front of the press gallery, to the annoyance of the other reporters. They have the same two seats today. Gradually the desire of politicians to have their words reported on radio overcame the old reserve.

Parliamentary reporting overall is obviously not quite as formal as it was, while the Friday reports, less laden with the need to report a full day's business in the Commons, can now spend time reporting the work of the select committees; the downside of this is a certain amount of lobbying of the unit by MPs to give more time to one committee than another. The work of select committees, as well as political work outside of Parliament, can be sensibly edited and interpreted, so tends to make much more sense to an outside audience than the mumblings too often heard within the Palace of Westminster.

Mark D'Arcy stresses in his book that his work for the Parliamentary unit calls for the functions of a theatre critic, a sports reporter and a political nerd. 'And for all the regular loose talk about the declining relevance of Parliament in an increasingly presidential political system, the Commons can still break ministers and defy governments' which involves 'murky concoctions of awkward principle, tribal loyalties, procedural manoeuvre and high drama'.

Well, he would, wouldn't he? The fact remains that, however big the audience may be for these (fairly) straight reports of daily business, a far bigger audience depends on the more lively, if sometimes confusing, analysis of political life produced by programmes covering news and current affairs, as politicians know very well.

Countryside

Britain is getting more like France, it seems. In France it has long been known to every person in a public position that you do not mess with the countryside, for the simple reason that it represents the soul of the nation, whether one lives in a slum, an apartment, a commune or else, just possibly, in the country.

The British used to be more pragmatic. For most of them, the countryside used to be a mildly pleasant place to visit from time to time, if only to experience the ire of the locals who resented your threat to their animals, their crops or their seat in the local pub.

All of this was reflected by Radio Four. Farming programmes were initially public service vehicles specifically for farmers, much as the shipping forecast is solely for those on ships. Their role was to report the latest prices for commodities, the latest threat to agriculture, the latest forecast of weather that could effect the production of food.

For as long as this was assumed, the more difficult it became to justify giving time and space to the subject. Farming got more efficient through the simple process of mechanisation and mergers, plus the laying off of manpower. The target audience got rapidly smaller. Other producers in Radio Four made claims for the use of the space.

However, public announcements of the intention to slim down farming programming produced an amazing number of complaints. Not from farmers who, by this time, had largely discovered other ways of collecting essential information, but from listeners who liked to start their day by breathing in country air, so to speak.

Britons had become more French.

BBC governors commissioned an enquiry. This produced the surprising information that, while the active farming population was falling by 20,000 a year, the number of people moving to live in the country (which covers 75 percent of our land area) was growing by 100,000 a year. This put a wholly new perspective on programming. Looking after the countryside, its birds and animals, became as important as producing food.

An editor was appointed with experience of wider news values, the news department attached a specialist reporter to the farming unit, and another reporter was also attached to concentrate on the environment – the new responsibility of farmers.

The growing number of programmes attracted a rapidly growing audience, including politicians when they needed to know of sensitive developments. Foot and mouth, bird flu and similar scares demand swift contact with rural areas and the expertise within the department has often provided a public service to more than the immediate audience.

The problem with having a wider brief is the greater number of interested parties who try to influence programme content. When I worked many years ago for Farmers Weekly the only NGOs were the National Farmers Union and the Soil Association, each of which were kept at a firm distance; now there are said to be something like six hundred, which clearly can cause congestion.

But all of this seems far away when one hears Dillon Winter in Open Country (one of the last outposts of the freewheeling, on site, conversational interview) being thankful for his job by declaring with glee as he trudges across the open land 'I ought to be paying to do this'.

Of course, On your Farm gives good value in providing an insight into how people say they are making a living from food, but I am always reminded of how much farmers keep their taxable cards very close to their chests. I personally believe that the strongest sniff of agriculture, if not agribusiness, often reaches Radio Four at the moment through Gardeners Question Time, when the panel of experts get to grapple with real plants, real soil and real weather conditions.

Fiction

Story-telling must surely be the purest form of radio. It harks back to the very beginning of civilisation, as an act of gathering together around a fire (or radio set) and listening to someone describe an event, factual or fictional, in such a way as to hold our attention, partly because of the convincing way the story is told, partly because we so strongly want it to be true. Such an experience activates the most distinctive part of being human, which is the ability to anticipate a future.

However, while story-telling enriches by helping to widen understanding, it can also threaten by detracting from what is often a more immediate need, to concentrate on the present. Hence, using fiction just as an occasional marker in the day has long been an established part of the Radio Four service.

The markers usually appear as a five day, fifteen minute

series in the early morning in the form of The Book of the Week, with another series of the same length late in the evening as A Book at Bedtime, and in the middle of the afternoon in a slot generically described as The Afternoon Story. The department responsible for these is currently called the audio music division, although it used to be called the radio music division. The logic of either title evades me. They are also responsible for an occasional series within Woman's Hour and for a few hours during the year on Radio Three.

Obviously, the choice of books has to be subjective, but there is a conscious aim to vary the subject matter, such as between mainstream and less conventional fiction and between old and new. There is normally one reader per book (of a heavily abridged version, of course) who is either the author or an actor, but there have sometimes been more than one, providing the budget allowed it.

A friend of mine had a book selected as The Book of the Week and was so determined to pass the test of being allowed to read his own words that he paid for a course of professional training, despite having what I would call a naturally good broadcasting voice. However, most writers are either not available or not suitable. I am sure we can all remember hearing painful recordings of poets from the past, drearily ploughing through their golden text, amazingly unaware that their audience cannot also read the words. Praise be for tactful producers.

The Book of the Week draws the biggest response from

listeners, and A Book at Bedtime the least. It is doubtful if this reflects less interest, so much that any sort of response is more difficult at that time. Of course, being read a story in bed before dozing off may be childish, but is all the same comforting.

Business

This is a sore subject for me. I have put a lot of effort over the years into trying to shake broadcasters into recognising the importance of the subject. I mean, we all work, or hope to work, for a living, so what more engaging a subject can there be?

However, for journalists it is not easy. Or, rather, it is easy when you can be thought to be tackling the subject so adroitly by reporting, say, the FT index, or the value of the dollar against the pound. However, when you ask broadcasters, as I have, to describe the relevance of the FT index or the dollar index to their average audience they are lost, partly because they don't understand the function of either indicator in the first place.

At least ITN news was persuaded to drop the dollar/pound index in favour of reporting on a wider monetary basket. But if you are not in the trading business it is of little interest anyway. The pound in your pocket is the pound in your pocket, as Harold Wilson would have said.

Not only broadcasters are to blame, of course. The average

newspaper shows very little awareness of the difference between doing business and investing in business. In my observation, few people do both. So they are different audiences.

At the Financial Times I used to frequently plot with colleagues on ways of launching a true business newspaper in the UK, perhaps something equivalent to the Journal of Commerce in the US. But technology overtook us. On-line business information has now supplanted newspapers in this context. This also explains how the long-running Financial World Tonight on Radio Four came to its natural end.

Anyway, the end result of all my campaigning has certainly been a growth in business journalism, but still of a kind that stresses investment (or gambling), rather than core business itself. The justification for this in newspapers is because this is where much of their advertising comes from, but that hardly applies to the BBC.

Hence, leaders of big public companies (representing a tiny share of British business) are usually wheeled onto the Today programme when their results are published, when they are only too happy to produce a few glib words of confidence and reassurance on the value of their organisation prepared by their advisers. There is very little talk about business. More usually, city analysts are asked to comment, for the sensible reason that they can add balance, but, again, only in terms of investment. The growing world of private equity, being private, is seldom reported.

Of course, the BBC in general is marvellous when it comes to economics. The full year and half year pronouncements from The Treasury and Bank of England are covered with extreme urgency and dedication to relevance. Even the mysterious workings of the international financial institutions are covered assiduously, despite the reporters usually forgetting to remind us of the purpose and relevance of these bodies. No doubt this is the result of recruiting staff with good degrees from good universities, where such stuff is taken for granted.

No, the sad fact is that, for Radio Four, real business coverage (of research, design, manufacturing, marketing, and all the other things we all do all day) is currently in the hands of just one man, Peter Day, whose occasional series of sensible weekly reports, although broadcast in the afternoons, all the same shed impressive amounts of light. Goodness knows what would happen without him. We'd get night instead of Day, perhaps?

Weather report

There are mainly two types of weather report on Radio Four. One is for general consumption, which has shrunk over the years. I seem to remember a full five minutes of detail at one time, when the script was left entirely to the people in the Weather Centre. Then a determined news editor decided to take a hand in it and instructions were issued on ways of editing five minutes of copy down to two, or not much more.

As far as I can tell, it seems to work well enough.

It is generally accepted that weather reports and traffic reports are the two most popular items on local radio stations, followed by the news, so the temptation is to make the most of them. As it is, the popularity of weather is used to draw the audience on national Radio Four into that slice of the hour which is designed to include a trailer for programmes to come. Clever that.

Something I understand less is the shipping forecast. I do understand that people at sea do need to know about potentially dangerous gales and so on, and that they may not always have their receivers tuned into long wave programming, so that an occasional shipping forecast on VHF and digital could come in very handy, but why can not this be edited down to two minutes, as well?

As it is, the full announcement may as well be delivered in Sanskrit, for all the sense it makes to those people who are not at sea. On the other hand, I am aware that Radio Four announcers consider it much as a Catholic priest considers a sermon in Latin: it is not the content that matters so much as the opportunity to master the mysteries of intonation.

Perhaps some listeners share this arcane appreciation.

Especially early on a misty morning.

Conversation

If anything crystallises intellectual excellence it has to be conversation. And there is nothing like good craic, as they say in Ireland. But craic means more than talk alone. It also means having a good time, possibly with the addition of music or jokes, or even food and drink. Obviously, listening to a good craic on the radio rules out sharing food and drink, at least by courtesy of the BBC, but the rest should be achievable. And is, my goodness.

The week starts with Start the Week, of course. This seems to have existed for ever, but I may have that impression because, for some while, it was a fairly pedestrian programme (even when I was working for it) and nothing drags more than a conversation where the listener is ahead of the speakers.

The ability to anticipate a line of thought is a gift not given to many, but the key role of facilitator in a discussion programme is as nothing without it. As is the ability to listen at the same time as thinking ahead. The former political reporter Andrew Marr manages this adroitly on STW at the time of writing, no sweat.

The point of STW, as with all the talk slots at nine in the morning through the week, is not to talk about the news, as that has already just happened exhaustively, so to speak, on the Today programme, but to talk about a far wider range of semi-topical events that allow for more than one or two points of view. The formula is one of interviewing a handful of subject specialists, then allowing them to question each other on the others' subjects. Lateral thinking to the fore, in fact.

The most challenging, yet rewarding, of all conversation

programmes is undeniably the Thursday slot for In our Time, presented by Melvyn Bragg. This transparent dissection of basic intellectual concepts is a pure joy to hear, as shown by the enormous demand for downloads, either from people who were not available to hear the programme when broadcast (or repeated later in the day), or else from those who want to keep hold of them for just that little bit longer.

Mind you, there are a number of listeners who find it a bit too challenging. Even Bragg had to end one session with the double-edged compliment to his panel of experts: 'Thank you for that. I've enjoyed it and I think I've understood a bit of it.'

The Wednesday afternoon slot Thinking Allowed (pun intended, I am sure) created by the impish enthusiasm of Laurie Taylor, is another source of intellectual cream for me, of the very highest quality. The fact that it is very much a one-man band can lead at times to a feeling of desperation when a theme does not quite come through, but that is rare. During broadcast, the hunger to reach further fields of greater understanding is curiously infectious.

The Saturday evening splurge of intellectual gamesmanship called Loose Ends, originally presented by that stalwart dramatic deviant Ned Sherrin is, in my opinion, suitably mischievous for a weekend, meaning good fun. While the morning slot called Saturday Live, presented by the impish Radio One escapee Fi Glover is almost too bright for such a time of day. On the other hand, it has fully filled the Home Truths hole left by the excellently droll but equally impish

John Peel, whose early death threatened to dampen radio on Saturday mornings for ever.

And how would anyone ever wake up on a Sunday without the forceful but friendly Broadcasting House, lacking only the sounds of a fully cooked breakfast?

I would even include a music programme in this section, namely Desert Island Discs. This inspired formula of asking people to name their eight favourite records, together with their reason for choosing them, has seldom, over many years, failed to reveal hidden truths, sometimes impressive, sometimes derisory. Simply demonstrating that people who are mostly presented as non-cultural entities can, in fact, have a cultural identity is always refreshing.

What I really cannot understand is how such a wealth of mental liveliness on the airwaves seems to have done nothing to lessen the tsunami of banality (I am on the train talk) that floods every public space in Britain with access to mobile phones. Ah well.

News

First, let's look at the mechanics. News is the backbone of the BBC and also of Radio Four. The operation is enormous. With over two thousand specific employees and 48 bureaux, 42 of them overseas, BBC News is the biggest news gathering operation in the world. And this does not include BBC Nations and Regions (strictly internal), nor BBC Global (strictly external), each of which buys into this supply but also produces material in its own right. This means that every year BBC News reports from over 150 countries and provides more than 45,000 hours of programming, converting into an average of 120 hours each day of the year, at an annual cost of £89.5m. Out of this Radio Four plucks 2,374 hours of news a year, which averages into 6.5 hours a day, of bulletins, programmes, whatever. I hope you are counting.

Digital technology has made possible enormous efficiencies, such as being able to use the same correspondent to deliver reports for use by television as well as radio, as well as for web pages. It has also led to a considerable increase in live coverage, which is just as well, considering that the delivery of programmes, including news, is also becoming more instant. An extra, if nervous, boost was given to the budget when, for a little while, world-wide competition from CNN looked potentially serious.

Correspondents for all news sections use English as a base language, which means that BBC Global, for instance, can translate reports for its various overseas services but works from the same core material as every other arm of the BBC.

As Radio Four also transmits (within Britain and wherever) 1,305 hours described as factual programmes a year and 1,194 hours called current affairs, it would be hard to draw a hard line between all three categories, if only because people who normally work in news would also at times contribute both themselves and their resources to these other streams.

Now let's look at the process. The value of being able to use your own, fully employed staff to report the news from difficult situations and distant places should not be underestimated. Only a full-time, professional news freak like me is likely to have a personal feel about this, but there are a lot of us; some of us in journalism, others in professions that depend on journalism to communicate with the world.

If a sudden event is reported from somewhere overseas you have never previously heard of, the odds are high that the first report will come through a news agency, such as Reuters, The Press Association or Agence France-Presse. If you are a news editor in London you then have to make an instant decision on how best to check it out and follow it up. If you have nobody on the staff within arm's reach, you need to look for a freelance correspondent. You are then dependent on someone who is probably not personally known to you and for whose veracity you cannot vouch. If you work for the BBC (sometimes also the Financial Times or Daily Telegraph) you contact your nearest available member of staff, who, obviously, you do know and can vouch for.

The difference in the quality of journalism is always obvious. It is not that journalists in other countries are not competent. It is simply the difference between Britain, where journalists are expected to be independent, and other countries where they are not.

The political, commercial, moral and legal pressures on journalists in other countries are always too easily forgotten.

Most British newspapers have no staff in any other country. This is where the BBC has an edge unrivalled in the world.

It would be nice to be able to depend on agencies. But after the national news agency Reuters (created by a German Jewish immigrant, Paul Julius Reuter, in 1851) was nationalised during WW2, it was passed by the government to the national press, who afterwards decided to accept the offer of a juicy management buyout. The national newspapers decided it was best (more competitive) if they each opened their own foreign bureaux.

When they afterwards realised that they had made an expensive mistake, it was then too late; Reuters had moved back to its original business of reporting finance, as banks pay better than papers. There still is a world-wide spread of offices, now fully equipped with video equipment, but income from news is marginal.

Generally speaking, the physical coverage of news by staff reporters is a shrinking function. Many newspapers are now driven by a mere handful of editors in head office, wherever that may be, who may have a considerable amount of knowledge and experience spread between them, plus a large quota of cynicism, but whose ability to establish the most likely truth of any contemporary claim, political, commercial, scientific or whatever, is strictly limited to whoever they can get on the phone in the next half hour that they can trust to do that for them. Some task. Some trust.

Within Britain alone the BBC has a contingent of 65 full-time home affairs specialists who monitor subjects such as home and legal affairs, education and family, culture, science and environment, health, community affairs, and royals and who work for no other master. Radio Four can draw on this as much as may be needed.

But so far we have been looking at hard news. Softer news, or factual background to topical issues that explains the background to current events, often depends on freelance reporters who have usually spent more time than others on the subject or in the area.

That excellently succinct programme From Our Own Correspondent would be hard pressed to provide two editions a week without a constant supply of material from independent journalists reporting from abroad, each of whom has developed a reputation for reliability in sometimes quite different media. Indeed, I think it fair to say that the majority of the most prominent broadcasters working for the BBC on any platform are not and never have been members of the BBC staff.

Of course, being the biggest news gatherer in the world does not guarantee being the best. We all have our complaints. Mine include the constant confusion in news bulletins between the European Court of Human Rights in Strasbourg with the European Court of Justice in The Hague. Also the ignorance of news editors who no doubt live in west London about the geography of east London; hence Romford is apparently in the east of the city, while Windsor is clearly not in its west. No doubt this is the kind of detail that the BBC's new, if virtual, college of journalism is addressing in its courses for staff.

More seriously, the under-reporting for many years of Palestinian issues in favour of Israeli, although denied, has probably had a serious effect on security in the Middle East. And there are many parts of the world, both inside and outside of Britain, which never get reported at all, partly because nobody has recognised the need, partly because there has to be a limit on the number of stories in bulletins.

This is another instance where other media have helped to set the trend. For instance, anyone regularly reading the well-informed Economist will not fail to notice how soon after its publication many of the same stories will appear in Radio Four bulletins. And in the same way as The Economist has gradually moved more into news stories in the areas of science and the arts, so have other media, including broadcasters. Other media have other effects.

Drama

I suppose drama is as far removed from news as you can get. To paraphrase an infamous US politician, it is not just about the things you know you don't know, but it is also about the things you don't know you don't know. On top of that, you can hear real people not knowing it but pretending to know it. It is fantasy put to a purpose, by stretching the borders of experience. And BBC radio drama has to be one of the strongest aspects of Radio Four, as it is, by my observation, one of the ingredients that most compels listeners to plan their day around it. They need perspective on real life. News may run from morning to night, but a play usually appears just once; miss it at your peril.

The fact that the drama output also provides a good living for a great number of actors in between their other occasional work clearly helps to enrich society. Also actors love the idea of not having to memorise their words, of not having to worry about how they look, of being able to whisper as well as project, of delivering just one, definitive, performance.

About thirty percent of drama output is produced by independent companies, but the rest, some 400 hours a year, is produced in house by a staff of eighty at an annual cost of about £8m. This is not a subject overwhelmed by audience participation. You do not have to agree or disagree with a play. You are involved or not involved. Which you might think would make the twice yearly process of commissioning, which happens across the whole of Radio Four, relatively easy for drama. Not so.

Since the introduction of external suppliers, commissioning editors have to balance the merits of internal against external proposals, albeit within the agreed quotas for each of them. This means that almost as much work has to be put into the proposal as would be put into the finished production and, bearing in mind that half of the proposals will not get approval, this means that an awful lot of time and money is virtually wasted. You could see this as a loss from the production budget. For a few years now the drama department has had the advantage over other departments of owning its production staff, meaning studio engineers who do nothing but drama, which clearly encourages a degree of sympathy and expertise which can only add to the finished product.

All the same, dealing in fantasy while slotting programmes into what is mainly a news and current affairs station clearly has the potential to produce conflict in getting approval for output. There is clearly some reluctance in the production team to put out what some people call faction, or the topical dramatisation of real events under the label of drama. On the other hand, if there is a perfectly good play available which happens to be set in a country which has been exhaustively reported in news programmes, there is likely to be discouragement from management.

But, without friction, there would be no drama.

Comedy

One man's joke is another man's poison, to coin a paraphrase. Hence, a comedy programme on radio that one person believes to be absolutely glorious can leave another person completely cold, if not outrageously offended.

Historically, BBC radio can be immensely proud of programmes such as It's That Man Again with Tommy

Handley, the Goon Show, Round the Horn and (Tony) Hancock's Half Hour. More recently, it can boast of The Hitchhikers Guide to the Galaxy, Goodness, Gracious Me, The League of Gentlemen, People like Us, Little Britain and Dead Ringers, all of which graduated to television.

Weekending was probably responsible for launching more writing and performance comedy talent onto the British Isles than any other programme, especially if the writers were conveniently London-based, with an enviable gift for swiftly levering the week's news into the stratosphere of re-context and absurdity, while anything produced by Frank Muir or Denis Norden is likely to have become an essential part of an introduction to real life for generations of teenagers. And Kenneth Williams. And Kenneth Horne.

A recent poll of listeners, albeit conducted by the BBC, to identify the most popular radio comedy programme put On the Hour firmly at the top, which is interesting insofar as it was distinguished by being what you might call the straightest of all comedy programmes, confusable with being a factual programme, with the humour obvious only if you listen carefully to the meaning of the words; not a single eccentric accent. In a similar style was a glorious spoof of 1066 and All That called 2066 and All That; straight enough to be as good as true. And then there are the golden oldies such as Quote Unquote, I'm Sorry I Haven't a Clue, Just a Minute and The News Quiz, driven almost blindfolded by the droll urbanity of old hands like Humphrey Littleton and Clement Freud.

However, there is the pressing awareness that younger voices must get in, perhaps not to drive down the age of the average listener so much as to, at least, not drive away new audiences. Most of us know of quite young people who listen to Radio Four only for the comedy programmes, if only introduced by their parents. So there are what seems to be at times an enormous number of truly awful programmes, with a generous superfluity of supposedly funny voices but with no real comedic conviction. I put it to the production head for radio comedy that, because of the very personal nature of humour, his was perhaps the hardest of all production jobs and he agreed, but also said that 'You have to kiss a lot of frogs to find a prince'. Laugh if you really want to.

With a production staff of 26 the head of comedy provides about 120 hours of material every year for BBC Radios 4, 2 and 7. On Radio Four he competes with outside companies to fill normally three spaces a day, at 11.30 am, 6.30 pm (when they hope to grab the youth audience before it locks onto television) and 11.30 pm. On average he succeeds two times out of three. The bidding process normally takes place six months before broadcast. Most of these bids are made only on paper, no doubt with an amount of personal description of the talent available. He would prefer to see more bids made in the form of pilot programmes, but this is generally not economic.

The problem with comedy is one of chemistry, which is very hard to see in a script. Situation comedies are easier, as they mainly depend on the character of the actors, who are usually already known, so you can imagine them reading the words. Others have to be taken on trust, so clearly must sometimes fail. But not everybody fails completely. Some series have had remedial treatment and have finally been made to work. Comments from listeners posted on the message board have sometimes provided the clue. While the number of downloads of any programme are proof of popularity.

Every so often the producers invite newcomers to try their hand at writing scripts and most that come back have the unmistakable stamp of a production contrived for the last year at school. Potential performers have usually done some stand-up comedy in front of a mainly male audience at comedy clubs, or a more mixed one at the Edinburgh Festival Fringe. As platforms, these are not exactly ideal for the existing audience of Radio Four, but they can still produce some real professionals, like Andy Hamilton and Jeremy Hardy and the late lamented Linda Smith.

Its no joke producing laughs.

Sport

There are few more frustrating experiences than having to listen to other people communicate in a foreign language. Close behind that, for me, is listening to people talk about what other people are doing. Voyeurism, I think it is called. Combine them both and what you have is sports reporting.

Although most people have little interest in sport, actively or passively, I happen to like running after a ball as much as anyone, especially if it is a squash ball and it is hit skilfully, but I prefer doing it to talking about it. And, if I do talk about it, I always try to explain to any existing audience what it is that I am talking about.

This seems unnecessary to most sports reporters. Surely, they believe, that if you announce that France beat England by four to three you are clearly talking about football. Or is it rugby? Or could it be hockey? And if Desert Star comes in first at the 2.45 at Doncaster are we talking about a horse, a greyhound, or a spaceship? Who cares? They don't. Hence, most of the audience for most of the time might as well be listening to a report in a foreign language, often relayed by someone who wasn't there anyway. (And how do you explain offside, birdie and silly mid-on?)

Come to that, who remembers that the phrase 'back to square one' dates from the days when the Radio Times provided a chart of a football field divided into squares, so that commentators could say where the ball had got to by quoting a number? Surely that shows how awkward sport is on radio?

The situation is this, I suppose. Every enthusiast is liable to both attract and repel others according to their ability to share his enthusiasm; and even if you know nothing of the enthusiasm or sport on hand, it is still possible to vicariously share another's enthusiasm if it is demonstrated with sufficient conviction; but only up to a point; after that it becomes frustrating. So sports reports on general programmes could just about be tenable for short periods of time, which is how it normally goes. Not to have them at all would run the risk of large numbers of sports enthusiasts migrating to another source, possibly permanently, and no programme controller would willingly risk that.

So that is why everybody who has little or no interest in sports will have to endure these reports, if that is what they are, for a long time yet.

On the other hand, if sports coverage were able to be broadened in some way, for instance to include Britain's most popular sport, which is fishing, or the enthusiasm of young Britons for particular sports such as swimming and table tennis, then the subject may become more welcome.

I must also admit that I seem to know a number of people who are fixated, often for impressive periods of time, on a mysterious and certainly inexplicable activity called cricket, which is said to be an integral part of Radio Four, but only on medium wave. As I have never knowingly owned a receiver capable of getting anything other than vhf or digital broadcasts, all of this is hidden from me. (But not from listeners in parts of Wales, where medium wave is all they have, so they have no alternative to hours and hours of cricket.)

However, my friends do their best to convert me, explaining that it is not the game itself that makes good radio, but the atmosphere created by the commentary. I don't get it. If there is any event undeniably done better on television than radio, apart from moon landings and coronations, it has to be sport, where the visual ambiance of the event is just as interesting as the main game and where words are so often redundant. Enough said.

Woman's Hour

This is an institution of its own. And very sensibly, too. Obviously it stems from the years of almost complete social separation of the sexes in Britain, when men were the bread-earners and women the home-makers, but war and economic pressure changed all that. In the same way as the social classes had to learn to mix together, so did the sexes, and the hard edges between them all were obviously smoothed.

But real changes of this kind normally have to wait for the next generation. As management consultants say, winning people over to new ideas is never a problem; convincing them to drop old ideas is.

In my post war days before broadcasting I can still remember failing to convince the editor of the Daily Telegraph that having the same report on the news pages as on the women's pages might possibly be a mistake: 'Oh, nobody reads the women's pages' he said. Later I was to become managing editor of a ground-breaking monthly woman's magazine, only to be told by a dismayed publisher that we had more male readers than female. Gender interests had certainly skewed.

But what man today has not pored over the pages of a woman's magazine in a vain attempt to understand a little better the mysteries of a woman's mind? And what man today, with access to Radio Four in the morning, can honestly say that he does not listen to Woman's Hour for very similar reasons? It is a kind of cross-gender buffet.

When it began, the programme was originally presented by a man, presumably because the (male) management thought that such a weighty task was not sufficiently lady-like. And there has nearly always been a man among the ranks of producers, presumably to make sure that no rash assumptions were made on air about the opposite sex. I knew one of these lucky men for some years and he was totally convinced that the sole reason for his appointment was his beard. Tokenism is not isolated.

Of course, there have been a number of vain attempts to start magazine programmes mainly for men. But it seems that they failed for exactly the same reason that general magazines for men fail – and I write, again, from professional experience. Men do not seem to have the same need to share their memories, their worries, their secrets with each other. Sex they understand, because that, like everything else, is something that you do, not talk about, isn't it? But if women continue to want a place where they can share their thoughts on what might be described as female interests, why not? It has even dealt with male issues at times. Well, somebody has to.

Once upon a time the programme went out in the afternoon, after a memorable short programme called Listen with Mother, directed at barely vocal toddlers.

I suppose the idea was to so exhaust the little darlings with concentrated attention that mother could afterwards put her feet up in peace, in order to consider more senior affairs. But broadcasting to a barely vocal audience clearly had its limitations, whereas what might be called the captive female audience was inevitably going to be bigger before, rather than after midday; so the first was dropped and the second was moved.

As far as I know, the programme is unique in every edition in extending the perspective of its multiple comparative analysis (or friendly chat, if you insist) even further forward before closing the meal by adding a creamy slice of fiction.

A diet for the mind, perhaps.

Arts

If the primary brief for everything on Radio Four is to be news oriented, then one department that has no problem with that nowadays is arts. There is so much going on in the world of art, especially in London where most of the programming happens, that the department has to come close to politics in being the recipient of more publicity material than it knows what to do with. Everything from jazz in churches to fireworks on boats to operas in old castles and films in college halls. Then there are still the big film releases and the big book publications and the final, final world tours of world famous artists. Writing as someone who has only marginally succeeded in profiling artists like Tom Stoppard and Bridget Riley, I am full of admiration for those who manage these things better. Not every art form or artist can have their rationale easily translated into a language which is accessible to all. Certainly the most news oriented arts programme is Front Row, which produces 260 programmes a year from Monday to Friday, which means having to fill 100 hours of airtime a month. The daily planning meeting is even called a news meeting.

Most programmes are a mix of ingredients, but they occasionally concentrate on single issues if the subjects are strong enough and if they have sufficient notice to be able to plan the necessary amount of work. Most programmes are also produced in the studio, but location reports can also be used, although with even more advance notice to arrange the mechanics, say five to six weeks.

Then I suppose everyone who reads likes to catch one or other of the book programmes when they can: Book Club, A Good Read, Open Book and so on. Even rediscovering old and neglected books can be a pleasure, although a growing number of us will have to search to find them on-line rather than blowing the dust off them in the attic.

And hearing real live authors explain their motivation to ordinary members of the reading public is a humanising experience, for us if not for them. And very occasionally, of course, there is Poetry Please. It would be interesting to know whether this adds to the actual sale of poetry. Just a little, perhaps.

Analysis

I am using this as a heading for a group of programmes. The Analysis programme itself, of course, has been going for some time and for many years had the field to itself. The imperious tones of Mary Goldring will still be etched, probably painfully, onto many people's eardrums. But it eventually became obvious that there was a large area of subjects not normally covered in this London-centric vehicle dominated by talking heads, so the Manchester studios were encouraged to launch a more inclusive alternative called File on Four, making more use of location interviews.

Eventually a whole array of regular programmes with different styles evolved on science, the media, philosophy, geography, history, law and so on. It has often occurred to me that degrees aught to be offered to long-term listeners, on receipt of proof that they had listened to and understood these programmes. Open University, good bye.

Perhaps the emperor of all analytical programmes is In Our Time, which seems to have a completely open brief to deal with any concept, providing it is sufficiently fundamental to be important yet so far generally ignored by the bulk of the population. But I have already dealt with this under the heading of Conversation, which just goes to show how difficult labelling can be.

In another way, From Our Own Correspondent seems to me one of the best of all analytical programmes, albeit concentrating on foreign affairs. These first hand accounts of life in other countries, usually illustrating how normal people deal with everyday affairs, can often provide a usefully sympathetic insight into the formal presentation of national interests that often confuse the news agenda. When I travelled more overseas I made an occasional input. I also contributed to a parallel UK programme called In Britain Now. There seems to be no Britain Now. I wonder what this means?

There has definitely been a move under the present controller of Radio Four to be more fleet of foot in programme terms in reacting to current issues, so that an analytical or dramatic treatment of news events can be put together in a matter of days, which nearly always beats the technical ability of television.

Obviously, as the variety of analytical subject matter has widened, it makes less sense here to examine the genre as an entity. There is no reason why they should be either like or unlike each other. All the same, it is interesting to notice how most of them have grown to follow the original Analysis pattern of inviting talking heads to a studio, rather than the File on Four pattern of reporting by walking around. As I have said before, my editor at The Economist made it clear that he never expected to see me in the office other than on press days when stories are being written, because 'The world is out there, not here'.

All the same, the breadth of subject matter, because it grows, is impressive. The eventual successor to Alastair Cook's admirably intimate Letter from America, A Point of View, seems to have justified its space with a spread of commentators, despite a painful start with the didactic Brian Walden. The Reith Lectures have also maintained an excellent standard of liberal challenge quite atypical of their namesake. You could also include programmes such as Unreliable Evidence, Word of Mouth, Between Ourselves, On the Ropes and Thinking Allowed, but some have already been mentioned here in other summaries.

I suppose the word analysis has become as useful to Radio Four as the word investigative used to be to newspapers: as (and if) journalism improves each word will eventually apply to all output.

&

PERSPECTIVE

Realpolitik

If you started now you would not start from here. That is the opinion of many Radio Four insiders. But that must be true of any institution and surely the best use of institutional history is to learn from experience.

So where is here? I suggest that here is Radio Four looking forward, but occasionally backward.

Looking forward consists of preparing mainly for 2017 when the BBC charter is up for renewal. This is the deadline by which the government needs to decide whether or not to allow the corporation to continue in business as before. The government will assume this responsibility partly on the grounds that somebody has to ensure the best use of the television licence fee and so it may as well be them.

But in principle, at least, the decision could equally well be taken by the licence payers themselves, who, after all, give their money to the BBC and not to the government. The tradition of the government controlling the main broadcaster was based, you will remember, on the principle of national security, when the limited amount of radio spectrum had to be divided in such a way as to safeguard space for the spooks. Now, with our present superfluity of communication systems and broadcasters, old-fashioned radio waves are no longer a matter of security concern. Mind you, whatever government is in power in 2017 may not take any notice of that. Quite understandably. Few of us like uncomfortable truths. And as no other governmental member of the 60 year old Council of Europe (which shelters the European Court of Human Rights) has ever fully observed its own principle recommendation (96 - 10) of keeping their hands off the media, especially the so-called public service broadcasters, there is little incentive there for the British government to do so.

However, in 2006 the Department of Culture Media and Sport had the bright, if bold idea of asking licence payers what they thought about it. Not, mind you, whether they wanted to decide the future of the BBC, but what they thought about paying the licence fee, now and in the future.

Largely, most people were happy to go on paying for the BBC in this way (possibly because the alternatives were not all that clear to them), and most of them were quite happy to pay more, not only for the present product, but especially for a future, improved product.

The present cost of a television receiving licence is £131.50. (Legally, if you use only radio and do not have a television you need pay nothing. Equally if you watch television on-line.) Most said they would be willing to pay an average of £138.24 for the existing output but as much as £162.66 if various improvements were made. When asked about specific services, however, they said an improved BBC would generally be seen as worth an average of £6.31 a month for television and £2.07 a month for radio. This compares with the present actual total monthly cost of £7.54 for the eight television channels and £1.17 a month for the ten radio stations, presently paid out of the television licence income.

Which is great news for radio, as this suggests that the average listener thinks that the radio output overall is worth about twice what it actually costs. And as fans of Radio Four tend to support it rather more strongly than do fans of other stations we can assume that they would be prepared to pay more than double for that. At the moment, Radio Four is allowed a share of just 2.2 percent of total BBC production costs, meaning £71.m out of £2,155.9m. However, the government sponsored survey did not ask the respondents to evaluate each station.

The public believes that Radio Four is worth at least twice what it costs

But wait a minute. Politicians will not give up as easily as that. Public opinion is not that important, is it? So this is when we need to look backwards.

We started the book with a reminder of when Winston Churchill became frustrated with the BBC, partly because he had been prevented from making radio broadcasts as a minor politician, and partly because he remembered the BBC insisting on explaining the motivation of the disruptive general strike in 1926. His fury was mighty but futile.

Some of us may also remember the frustrations of another prime minister, Anthony Eden, during the illegal Suez Canal invasion of the 1950's. Eden decided to make a statement to the nation and was enraged when the BBC then agreed to allow the leader of the opposition, Hugh Gaitskill, to broadcast an opposing and protesting reply - on the grounds of political balance.

Eden believed he was speaking as the leader of the British government, not as a political spokesman. Hence the story began (and continued for a long time after) that he had consulted lawyers on taking total control of the corporation. However, as the rumour seems to have started on the pages of The Listener, a weekly then published by the BBC, it is not hard to see this as a bit of counter-intelligence.

More recently, there was the pressure on all broadcasters by the government of Margaret Thatcher during the latest Irish troubles to ban the voices of IRA members and even supportive and elected politicians, leading to the absurd (and more dramatic) process of interviewing them with their voices dubbed by professional actors. This lasted from 1988 to 1994 and was empowered by section 29 (3) of the Broadcasting Act of 1981, which effectively allows the government the last word in all matters of broadcast editorial dispute. It had never happened before and, so far, has not since. The National Union of Journalists challenged the action at the European Court of Human Rights, but failed, on the grounds that ensuring security overrides the right to free speech, even for elected politicians. There is no

There have been a number of attempts by politicians to influence BBC programmes

such law affecting print media.

Much more importantly and much more recently, as indicated right at the start of this book, it is pressure from contemporary politicians on an ongoing and unpredictable basis which always creates the greatest concern.

Of course, the problem is not one of (direct) censorship so much as (indirect) self-censorship. Up until 2007 this was evidenced in the BBC mainly by the membership of the 12 person board of governors. Although in theory established to guarantee the independence of the corporation by ensuring its self-governance, in practice the board members were appointed by the government, while the governors appointed the director general. This inevitably produced a body of opinion weighted in favour of the governing establishment and which most recently resulted in the wasteful resignation of both the chairman and the director general after the WMD/Gilligan/Kelly/Hutton affair. Personally I would describe this as the most severe attack ever on what I believe to be Britain's most important social enterprise, meaning Radio Four.

You will remember that the BBC (Radio Four's Today programme specifically) was *not* wrong to break the news that there were no weapons of mass destruction in Iraq (as the reporter Andrew Gilligan said he was told by the British government adviser, Doctor Kelly) but *was* wrong in reporting (once, at seven in the morning) that the government as a whole *knew* it was lying when it said that there were. All the same, Gavin Davis the chairman and Greg Dyke the director general were 'allowed' to resign by the board of governors for this offence; and subsequently a number of senior managers found themselves in different jobs. Lord Hutton's report of his enquiry into the death of Doctor Kelly was published in 2004 and only succeeded in making matters worse by delivering an extremely partial account of the events that led to the public identification and vilification of Doctor Kelly. In effect it said that the government had behaved properly and that the BBC had not, even though the release of Dr Kelly's name by the government was believed by many to have led to his death.

The departure of Greg Dyke had brought the staff out onto the streets. The government, as far as we know, had not specifically asked for this dramatic outcome, but the governors gave it to them, all the same. Which might be seen as a classic demonstration of self-censorship, despite the Queen's own words in the most recent BBC Charter saying 'We believe it to be in the interests of Our People that there should be an independent corporation'.

Perhaps the main compensation for this debacle was to witness the deft dissolution of the board of governors soon afterwards and its replacement by what is called the BBC Trust, which is also government appointed and appears to be little different to its predecessor but which may prove to be. Some of the previous governors' duties have been delegated to a new board of management and an effort has been made to draw a line between them and the Trust. Only time, and pressure, will tell how successful this will be. On the other hand, many would have been pleased to see that the man conspicuously at the centre of attacking the BBC, Alastair Campbell, the prime minister's volatile spokesman, stood down after the Hutton report, followed eventually by the prime minister himself, if only partially because of the Iraq debacle. But whether all of this frantic dropping out is good either for the government or the country is severely open to doubt. Not long after this affair, in September 2006 the committee of ministers of the Council of Europe issued yet another statement on the Europe-wide situation, saying 'Reportedly, in some cases, while relevant provisions [to ensure the independence of public service broadcasters] may be adequate, they are disregarded in practice, leaving [the organisation] under the effective control of the government or political bodies or formations, serving the interests of those bodies rather than society at large.' As in Albania, so in Britain. I suggest.

International agreements on the freedom of media have long been ignored by all governments

The most powerful light shone on this disgraceful state of affairs was from Boris Bergant, the deputy director general of the Slovenian public broadcaster, in Edinburgh in 2006 at the annual congress of the International Press Institute. Specifically: 'Politicians in many European countries still do not distinguish between public and state broadcasting . . . Some political groupings believe that since they are democratically elected majorities they also have the right to rule and influence public service broadcasting . . . There are dozens of important and strong political documents of the United Nations, UNESCO, Council of Europe and even the European Parliament safeguarding the political independence of PSB, but there are no practical and politically binding methods of monitoring and sanctions . . . Is it not strange that in the process of an accession of a given country to the Council of Europe or European Union the media relations are deeply scrutinised . . . but then, after a certain country is a member, nobody really cares?' As in Slovenia, so in Britain, it seems.

Lawyers in Europe have suggested some alternative supervisory structures for what are still called public service broadcasters, such as having trustees appointed by civil society groups, or else by a body including a balance of political parties. This does not seem ideal, but at least it moves the debate on.

The latest dictat took licence money away from the BBC and gave it to a competitor

More recently the government decided that the money that we pay the BBC is not just for the BBC, but for anything else they decide. So they ordered that £14m of the licence fee income collected by the BBC should be given to Channel Four to help pay their costs towards the imminent digital conversion process. After this it is only a small step to say that the licence fee should also be given to independent programme producers, as well as to other so called public service broadcasters, such as ITV, Five and S4C; a not unreasonable idea, but another one on which those paying the tax have not been consulted.

However, it seems possible that, with a bit of public help, the government may soon be moving in the right direction. A House of Lords committee in August 2007 ruled that the system of appointing the key figure of the BBC chairman was wrong, partly because it was invisible, but mainly because it was finally controlled by a government minister. Together with a deal of similar business which has lately been moved from Downing Street to Westminster, they say that this decision should also be controlled by members of parliament as the public's elected representatives.

Meanwhile, there's a new kid on the block. In 2003 a number of broadcasting regulators were merged into one called the Office of Communications (Ofcom), with powers that overarch both the mechanics of communication and the content. At the time this seemed a really useful way of tidying up the supervision of a divided but fast evolving sector. So for the first time an external body has a degree of supervision over the BBC; in this context it can study unresolved complaints from the public about such things as offensive or harmful material and it can order the broadcast of its findings; complaints about a radio programme must be made within three weeks of broadcast.

Ofcom's views were taken on board when BBC governors were replaced by the Trust. Ofcom also feels strongly about the need to plan for the next BBC charter. While substantially supporting the latest charter, they said 'Securing the BBC is not the same as securing public sector broadcasting for the future', especially once everyone has moved from analogue to digital reception. They argue for PSB to be adopted by many more broadcasters than at present and believe that a special fund should be created to help make this happen, possibly by adding a few pounds to the television licence fee. They also said that plans for this should be completed by 2010. No doubt they were mindful, among other things, of their plan to award a licence for a second national digital radio network to start broadcasting before then, by 2008.

At the same time, more people are buying computers and subscribing to broadband, and fewer people are watching television, especially in London. Nevertheless the audience for Radio Four holds remarkably steady, as more people are working from home, as well as living longer and, being better educated, they demand sound information and strong inspiration, which they are generally not getting from the shopping catalogues now called newspapers.

&

Competition

The dogs of war are barking, it seems. Radio Four expects competition. Not directly, but on different platforms.

When I started to write about media thirty years ago my editor suggested that in the next century people would be printing their newspapers out of their televisions and I did not believe him. Not for the first time I was wrong, but he was absolutely right inasmuch as computer terminals for many people have become, to a degree, the equivalent of televisions. And anyone can print from these, of course.

Also, the way in which people write messages has continually evolved, if only because of the nature of the medium. The Ten Commandments, brief and to the point, were written on stone; The Bible, more poetic, was written on parchment; The Book of Common Prayer, complex and ornate, was written on paper and now anything off the internet on whatever seems fit for the purpose.

Equally the way in which less literate people communicate has evolved. Smoke signals were followed by drums, semaphore, the Morse Code, telephone, radio, television, and so on. And you will remember from the first chapter how broadcasting began in Hungary via telephone, to where it now seems to be returning.

Considering audio communication alone, since the birth of Radio Four we have seen the birth of digital broadcasting and broadband on the world wide web. And people can listen to Radio Four on analogue or digital radio receivers, through digital television, on line through computers and then through MP3 players, as well as on mobile phones. And this is not just theory. As of 2006 two thirds of all British households had access to the internet, with half of all households using broadband and owning two mobile phones.

In essence this means that three in ten people listen to radio through the internet, over four in ten through digital television and one in five through a digital music player. While one in eight listen through a mobile phone with a built-in tuner, rising to one in three among 18 to 24 year olds. And they, of course, over time will age and mature into Radio Four listeners.

Already a fifth of radio listening happens without an analogue receiver

The result is that nearly a fifth of radio listening already happens without the traditional analogue receiver, with about the same number opting to listen to programmes after their scheduled broadcast times.

But content will always be king in journalism, and it is hard to see how any competitor can develop a reputation sufficiently strong to compete with the present Radio Four.

On one hand, you can look back to the emerging London Broadcasting Company, which was certainly eager to meet the Today programme head-on in the key London area. I remember. I was there. But it was a long and, finally, fruitless task. However skilled your staff may be, the really heavy-weight interviewees are not going to put themselves out for a still slender and un-influential audience. And without the speakers you do not get the audience.

On the other hand, you can look back to the birth of ITN news, and then Channel Four news. These each started with a considerable existing audience and then for many years, in effect, out-BBC'd the BBC, in terms of solid content and authoritative delivery. So nothing is impossible.

And the growing number of ways in which to reach that highly desirable target audience of older, influential and richer listeners which is Radio Four, whether it is fixed in time or on the move, certainly makes the task of competing less direct, so perhaps more flexible.

Most people believe that the down-loading of radio programmes generally onto MP3 players is going to grow, both in terms of demand and supply, aided by the fact that additional broadcasting rights for radio programmes, when compared with video and television, are comparatively easy to negotiate.

Some people in the business have been looking across the Atlantic at the well-established if not yet very prosperous business of delivering radio exclusively by satellite. At the time of writing there are two dominant systems, Sirius and XM, which have been trying to get US federal permission to boost income by joining forces with each other. Each of them charge largely car-bound listeners $12.95 a month for being able to access over 100 channels of music, sport, talk and other content.

Many of these channels are free of advertising and require a specific (and quite pricey) receiver, but these have already been fitted in all kinds of vehicles, from passenger planes to hire cars. In Europe, Asia and Africa we have a similar system in place called Worldspace, although obviously using different satellites. Sirius and XM also feed radio on-line.

Having watched this happening for some years, the BBC has now decided to launch a British satellite platform, Freesat, in conjunction with commercial broadcasters, exactly as it did with Freeview in order to head off Rupert Murdoch's SkyTV. Also like Freeview, the plan is to provide programming free of charge, although there would be a one-off charge for equipment supply and installation. The completion date is still in the sky, so to speak.

In an increasingly competitive media world, a major consolation for the BBC is that of expertise, of ability and experience of making good programmes. The next national digital terrestrial network in Britain has already been awarded to an offshoot of Channel Four, which has formed a partnership with a number of input providers. Although there is no indication of programme content, they say they will be aiming at 30 to 54 year olds, which is younger than Radio Four, of course.

During the bidding process the Financial Times was named

as a probable partner, although they were not part of the final offer. Which reminds me of my own time at the FT, working in what was optimistically called Business Enterprises, which was responsible for such things as newsletters and on-line information for British Telecom. It was not good. It seems to be in the nature of major publishers to believe that all other media is peanuts and that anyone can produce it. Hence the FT failed to provide the necessary management skill and support. Hence there was seldom anything but large losses. A similar situation is said to rule at the US satellite companies Sirius and XM.

The racing feet of competition have to move on the sands of changing media

As we have already seen, ensuring a proper marriage in journalism between management and the necessary creative forces is a hard task and seldom achieved. And launching an almost direct competitor to Radio Four on what is to be called Channel 4 Radio would seem extremely ambitious. However, there is no doubt that the BBC remembers those times in the past when it was outpaced by competitors, so is now determined to adopt any suitable new technology before anyone else; exactly as Freesat demonstrates.

Yet the hard question remains of how, in future, to make all of this pay. By the time the Royal Charter is up for renewal the number of conventional television receivers requiring licences may well have shrunk and, however eager the public may now be to pay for what they get from the BBC, their enthusiasm may then be less. After all, in the face of an ever richer media landscape, they will not be using their television sets so much. And they may well be paying substantial amounts for alternative and more specific services, by satellite or whatever. Already mobile phones are available that can receive FM radio. It would be only a small step to enable reception of digital broadcasts, together with the use of the screen to display text about the programme content. Once again, that elusive youth audience, much addicted to mobile phones, seems closer to the BBC grasp.

On the other hand, Radio Four listeners are not like others. Whether they are wiser may be open to dispute, but they are certainly older, and their subsequent reluctance to jump at the latest technology may mean that most of them will still be listening to their favourite station in real time for some years to come.

Nevertheless, come the next Charter, the BBC could very likely be sharing its licence fee with an increasing number of other broadcasters - and possibly programme makers - with a public service brief.

And alongside all this, little Radio Four, scraping along with just 2.2 percent of the total BBC production budget, despite its superior reach and influence, seems committed to its fate as a poor relation. This is not what the public expects.

&

Strategy

Better to cry wolf before the wolf arrives, I think. Better also to prepare a plan of action. The main problem with doing that for Radio Four is that it is part of a family, and a very large one at that.

Not surprisingly, the family are not keen on any individual member suggesting that he might be adding more value to the family than others, however true that may be, and especially not keen on that member indicating, therefore, that he would quite like to set up house on his own, or be dealt with as a special case.

Quite apart from that, the people who work for Radio Four are there largely because they want to be part of that bigger family, if only because of the flexibility it offers in terms of their future employment. It is in their interests to keep their heads down and, if necessary, to genuflect to senior family members.

However, the reality is that, from the public's point of view, Radio Four does stand apart from the rest of the BBC within Britain, primarily because it does not compete with, so does not need to react to, any commercial network. It is just this competitive pressure that has so recently led to the messy situation on BBC television with on-air game shows, where the results were shown to be rigged. The whole of the BBC is blamed for this, simply sharing guilt by association. And when public opinion is sought by pollsters, they never think of asking specifically of the **likely** involvement of radio output, or of Radio Four in particular, as the BBC has seemed to work so hard at getting the world to ignore it. Or, at least, has not worked to prevent it.

Equally, most published literature for the past twenty years on the BBC has almost totally ignored radio output, despite its obviously greater importance in every statistical way: a bigger audience, more influence. And then, of course, while the national media are keen to monitor television output, if only because they are competing for advertising, they almost totally fail to report on radio, despite the greater size of its audience.

In reality, talk radio, Radio Four, is enormously important. In print, it is practically invisible. Such are the problems of belonging to a family where the younger sons, who spend most money, get all the parental attention.

So who should do what?

There is probably no linear solution. At the end of the day, only politicians can do anything about sorting out the legislation, so that the BBC as a whole becomes as independent of government as its charter says it is and as the Council of Europe says it ought to be. This will probably mean forgetting about any successors to the old board of governors and passing the whole machinery of supervision over to Ofcom – after first ensuring legislation that equally ensures that Ofcom is independent. A good example has already been established with the Information Commissioner, who has as much independence as a High Court judge and can thus be dismissed only by passing new legislation.

However, politicians will not willingly sacrifice their leverage on the BBC without due reason, of course. And the only reason that carries weight with politicians is the opinion of the voting public.

This is where only the BBC can look after its own. After all, it does a marvellous job every few years in helping to ensure that its charter is renewed and, most importantly, that the licence fee is increased roughly in line with the rising cost of living. Indeed, this is not done just on a piecemeal basis. It is continuous. Behind the scenes, but continuous. It also does not do too badly in responding to erratic attacks on the standard of its output by publicity-seeking junior MPs. So the skill is there.

But at the end of the day both the BBC and those informed politicians who care would need the public to tell them what to do. And the public will not be able to do that without all of the available information.

This book is a bid to get the conversation going.

&

Credits

I have pretended that this book is all my own work. Now is the time to own up. The inspiration is due to all those who have ever asked me to explain in person what I have now tried to explain in print. They are far too many to remember, I am afraid.

The others who have since helped me to produce the book fall into two camps: the past and present BBC insiders who have so generously shared their knowledge and pooled their impressions; and those who are totally addicted as listeners to Radio Four and have read my work for both sense and relevance. There are members of both groups who disagree with my views, which is only to be expected. However, this is a list of both camps together, as so many people seemed to put stuff in as well as take it out.

Mark Damazer, Jock Gallagher, Elizabeth Smith, Kevin Marsh, Gerry Mansell, Stephen Whittle, Paul Hodgson, John Cain, Marshall Stewart, Andrew Caspari, Richard Sambrook, Monica Sims, Simon Coates, Denis Nowlan, Jim Black, Rick Thompson, Andrew Thorman, Alison Hindell, Peter Roberts, Mike Stock, Peter Knowles, Paul Schlessinger, Di Spiers, John Goudie, Christine Morgan, Russel Chant, Leigh Aspin, Simon Nelson, Peter Davis, Sue

Timothy, Tim Cheatle, Celia Hampton.

And none of this would have been possible without the hundreds of books and other reports already produced about the BBC, all of which I have shamelessly plundered and the best of which I have already credited.

Any mistakes are, of course, all mine.

London, November 2007

&

ETC

The service licence

The new BBC Trust, in reinforcing its role as supervisor rather than manager, has begun by issuing what are called service licences to the various broadcasting stations. Broadly, these are the proscribed aims and purposes for each service, described as encapsulating a recognisable sense of their DNA. I suspect that John Reith would have admired this, but that William Haley would not. In the public relations business such generous documentation is called Evidence of Effort.

Part 1: Key characteristics of the service
1. Remit
The remit of Radio 4 is to be a mixed speech service, offering in-depth news and current affairs and a wide range of other speech output including drama, readings, comedy, factual and magazine programmes.
The service should appeal to listeners seeking intelligent programmes in many genres which inform, educate and entertain.

2. Scope of the Licence
Radio 4 should be available every day for general reception in the UK on FM, Long Wave, Medium Wave in some parts of the UK, DAB digital radio and digital television platforms and it may be simulcast on the internet.

The service may offer its programmes streamed on-demand for a limited period after broadcast. It may also offer broadcast radio content for download for an unlimited period of time after broadcast, although this must not include unabridged readings of published works nor full track commercial music nor classical music (even if recorded by the BBC), and other interactive station and programme-related content via
bbc.co.uk. Broadcast audio programmes may be visually enhanced.

3. Service budget
Radio 4 has a service budget of £76.7 million in 2007/08.
This may be adjusted annually for Retail Price Inflation. Any planned or actual change in annual expenditure on the service of more than 10% in real value requires approval from the BBC Trust and may entail variation of this Service Licence.
1 Radio 4 currently offers a limited amount of mainly speech content on-demand for an unlimited time period after initial broadcast. Any expansion of the scope of this requires the approval of the BBC Trust.
2 Download of classical music in the form of incidental music or signature tunes is permitted.
3 This may include video related to output created for BBC broadcast, but should not include the commercial purchase of unrelated video rights.

4. Overview of aims and objectives
Radio 4 programmes should exhibit some or all of the following characteristics: high quality, original, challenging, innovative and engaging, and it should nurture UK talent.
Radio 4 should deliver its remit by providing in-depth news and

current affairs, strongly supported by a wide range of other speech programmes including politics, religion and ethics, history, science, documentaries, arts, literature, drama and readings, sports (subject to rights ownership) and comedy.

Accurate, impartial and independent news and current affairs should form the core of the output with a mix of daily news programmes and hourly news bulletins, investigative journalism, documentaries and debates, covering a very wide range of domestic and international issues. Domestic coverage should reflect the diversity of the UK.

The service should take risks and invest in original content rarely found elsewhere.

There should be a strong emphasis on original drama, readings and innovative comedy from new and established talent. The station should occasionally schedule special projects and seasons that explore particular themes or mark significant events or anniversaries.

It should make use of its availability on Long Wave to split the schedule at times, providing live coverage of major events, religious services, reports from Parliament, or sporting fixtures on one frequency while continuing to offer the main schedule on the other.

Radio 4 should make its high quality content available on digital platforms and promote DAB and other digital technologies to its audiences.

The broadcast output should be supported by a complimentary online service, including some use of visual enhancements, and listeners should be encouraged to interact and communicate with the station. Radio 4 should use new technology to ensure its audiences have the maximum opportunity to access programmes as and when they want.

Radio 4 should contribute to BBC Radio's commitment to commission some output from outside the M25 area and from independent producers.

When Purpose Remits have been adopted by the BBC Trust in 2007, this Service Licence will set out how this service will contribute to the promotion of relevant priorities set out in Purpose Remits.

Part II: Contribution to public value

5. Contribution to the promotion of the BBC's public purposes

5.1 Sustaining citizenship

Radio 4 should make a very important contribution to this purpose amongst its audience, through in-depth, accurate, impartial and independent news and current affairs output which should seek to enable listeners to participate more actively, critically and constructively in the democratic life of the UK. Extensive context should be provided, and leading figures from all areas of British life should be challenged over their policies and actions. At least once a week there should be live debates that include public participation. Investigative journalism should aim to uncover injustices, expose issues of concern and ask searching questions of those in positions of responsibility.

Radio 4 should provide daily reports of Parliamentary proceedings when Parliament is sitting. During local and general elections, it should provide impartial, rigorous and substantial analysis of the political parties' campaigns and issues of interest to listeners.

The schedule should offer regular coverage of subjects such as consumer affairs, education, health, business, law, farming and disability.

Radio 4 should:

Broadcast at least 2,500 hours of news and current affairs programmes each year.

5.2 Stimulating creativity and cultural excellence.

Radio 4 should make a very important contribution to this purpose amongst its audience. It should commission a significant amount of its programming from a range of suppliers.

The schedule should offer a wide range of drama including plays, serials and adaptations. Some writers commissioned should be new to radio. There should be regular readings of fiction, non-fiction and poetry. Exploration of literature and the arts should be a regular feature of the station.

Radio 4 should be the home of BBC radio comedy and make significant investment in developing new writing and performing talent and new comedy programmes.

Radio 4 should:

Broadcast at least 730 hours of original drama and readings each year.

Ensure that at least of 25% of new Afternoon Plays will be first or second commissions from writers new to radio.

Broadcast at least 180 hours of original comedy each year .

Contribute to BBC Radio's commitment to commission at least 10% of eligible hours of output from independent producers

5.3 Promoting education and learning

Radio 4 should make a very important contribution to this purpose amongst its audience by providing informal learning opportunities across a wide range of subjects.

It should seek to deepen and broaden listeners' understanding through specialist programmes on subjects such as politics, business, law, finance, health, education, food and farming, international affairs, religion, ethics, travel and gardening. There should be regular exploration of the sciences, including natural history and medicine.

History should be explored through biographical programmes, longer narrative series and one-off features and documentaries.

Radio 4 should support pan-BBC social action and educational campaigns where appropriate. It should also seek partnerships with organisations outside the BBC to extend the reach and impact of the station's education and learning output.

Radio 4 should:

Broadcast at least 200 hours of original documentaries each year.

5.4 Reflecting the UK's nations, regions and communities

Radio 4 should make an important contribution to this purpose amongst its audience.

Its journalism should reflect the diversity of the UK. Through its documentaries and features, Radio 4 should explore ethnic, cultural and religious groups within the UK, enabling the wider community to understand their customs, convictions and concerns. The station should also provide worship, celebration and in-depth reporting of religious affairs across all the major faiths. Radio 4 should provide live coverage of significant state events, enabling people across the UK to share a sense of unity.

This includes expenditure on first-run originated programming, but does not include expenditure on news or sport output.

Radio 4 should facilitate and support the growth of communities of interest around its output and enable them to interact with programmes and with each other online.

Its news and consumer programmes should cover stories of relevance to people with disabilities and there should be a weekly programme dedicated to issues for the blind and visually impaired.

Radio 4 should contribute to BBC Radio's commitment to ensure that at least one third of relevant expenditure is incurred outside the M25 area each year. Each week the schedule will include programmes from one or more of the English regions, Scotland, Wales and Northern Ireland. It should also commission output from independent companies based throughout the UK.

Radio 4 should:

Broadcast at least 200 hours of original religious programming each year.

5.5 Bringing the UK to the world and the world to the UK

Radio 4 should make an important contribution to this purpose amongst its audience, primarily by bringing the world to the UK through extensive and wide-ranging coverage of international issues and events in its journalism and other factual output.

Both regularly scheduled and one-off programmes should be used to explore international issues in considerable depth.

5.6 Emerging communications

The BBC's sixth public purpose is defined in the Charter as 'in promoting its other purposes, helping to deliver to the public the benefit of emerging communications technologies and services and, in addition, taking a leading role in the switchover to digital television'.

Radio 4 should contribute to the promotion of this purpose in a variety of ways which are described in this Service Licence.

6. Annexes to this Licence

6.1 Annex I – Performance assessment

The performance of Radio 4 will be assessed by the Trust using the framework described in Annex I. Radio 4's compliance with any Conditions, as described in section 5, will also be measured on an annual basis and reported in the Annual Report and Accounts.

The BBC Trust will expect Radio 4 to comply with the commitments described in sections 4 and 5 of the Service Licence. The BBC Trust will monitor compliance with these commitments retrospectively as part of its periodic service reviews and/or on an exceptional basis if there is evidence or allegation of non-compliance.

7. Operation of this Licence by the BBC Trust
For details of how the BBC Trust operates this Service Licence, please see the Service Licence Operating Framework. This is available from www.bbc.co.uk/bbctrust or upon request from the BBC Trust Unit.
Annex I: Performance measurement framework
The BBC Trust has the function of assessing the performance of the Executive Board in delivering the BBC's services and activities and holding the Executive Board to account for its performance. It will use the framework described below as the basis for its assessment of Radio 4.
The framework is based around the four drivers of public value: Reach, Quality, Impact and Value for money and it includes measurement of the five content characteristics, as described in the BBC Agreement: high quality, challenging, original, innovative and engaging.
The Trust can amend this framework without this constituting formal variation to this Service Licence.

Performance measurement framework
Reach: Radio 4 should contribute towards the maintenance of combined BBC weekly reach at over 90% by aiming to maintain its own weekly reach.

It should contribute towards on-demand consumption of content. This will be measured by weekly reach of non-DRM audio downloads over the internet.

Quality: audience approval of Radio 4 and perceptions of it as high quality and innovative. Also, the proportion of originated programmes across all hours. Impact: audience perceptions of Radio 4 as informative, engaging and challenging.

Value for money: Radio 4's cost per listener hour.

&